REINVENTING
Worship

**Prayers, Readings, Special
Services, and More**

B R A D B E R G L U N D

JUDSON PRESS
PUBLISHERS SINCE 1824
VALLEY FORGE

Reinventing Worship: Prayers, Readings, Special Services, and More
Brad Berglund

Library of Congress Cataloging-in-Publication Data

Berglund, Brad.
    Reinventing worship : prayers, readings, special services, and more / Brad Berglund.
        p.   cm.
    ISBN 0-8170-1493-4 (alk. paper)
    1. Worship programs. 2. Public worship. I. Title.
    BV198.B44   2006
    264—dc22
                                                                    2006006803

Printed in the U.S.A.

13 12 11 10 09 08 07 06

10 9 8 7 6 5 4 3 2 1

Contents

On Using This Resource and the Accompanying CD

All of the prayers, litanies, and other worship resources found in this book have been stored on the accompanying CD-ROM in ways that most, if not all, churches can access for easy use in bulletins or for projection onto a large screen. In addition to the content of this book, the CD includes 430 topically arranged readings from Scripture representing several different translations, most of them contemporary.

This book contains a variety of format styles with regard to the use of italics, bold typeface, and more. The CD provides churches with the ability to format the selections according to their own preferences.

Individual churches should feel free to make stylistic adjustments in order to make the material as user-friendly as possible in their ministry context. Please note, however, that the CD is to be used only by those who purchased this resource; it may not be reproduced.

Introduction

A church congregation or body of believers is in many ways like a person. It can be vital, creative, strong, ambitious, growing. Or it can be weak, confused, stagnant, joyless, perhaps even dying. Most church congregations fall somewhere between these two extremes. They are more vital than they might be, but not as vital as they could be.

One mark of a healthy church is a striving for increased vitality. The healthy congregation is not content with the status quo. Its people want to grow—spiritually, intellectually, and in various other ways, including numerically. To achieve this growth, the typical church adopts and implements a variety of programmatic emphases, ranging from the welcoming of visitors to new-member Bible studies to youth programs to community outreach ministries. Unfortunately, worship too frequently gets lost in this mix. As one of several components of congregational life, worship is sometimes assigned a low priority by church leaders and laypersons alike. Thus its potential for renewing and transforming church life goes unrealized.

In fact, vital, meaningful worship may be the most underrated element of healthy congregational life. People choose to try a particular church for a variety of reasons: denominational loyalty, location, youth programs, the preaching, and more. But no matter the reason people first choose to attend, they will find it hard (if not impossible) to leave the church if their lives are being renewed and changed—if they are experiencing meaningful encounters with God on a regular basis.

Worship has played a more central role in some church traditions than in others. But even in denominations that have emphasized worship, individual congregations are dying, as worship has become something of a lost art. In many instances, the routine of worship has become an end in itself, as opposed to a means to the end of encountering God.

The purpose of this volume is to provide resources for worship leaders to help individuals and congregations to experience worship as a life-changing experience, as opposed to mere routine. The resources herein represent both the theological and the stylistic diversity of the contemporary church; thus not every offering will be appropriate for every church, though the hope is that a high percentage will be.

Part of God's plan for the church is that we live in community. The worship service provides the one regular opportunity for the whole community to gather as one to be the church of Christ and to encounter the most holy God. My hope is that this resource will serve to accomplish this purpose.

Leading Worship

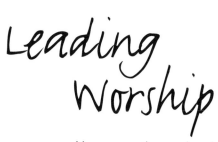

I have seen the sun break through
to illuminate a small field
for a while, and gone my way
and forgotten it. But that was the pearl
of great price, the one field that had
the treasure in it.

—R. S. Thomas, from "The Bright Field"[1]

People come to worship for a variety of reasons—to see friends and catch up on the events of each other's lives; to enjoy the music of the choir, worship team, or soloists; to learn something new; to go out for lunch after worship with a favorite group of people; and on and on. These important values, woven into the fabric of our worship routine, keep us busy, entertained, and even happy. If you made a list of the things you look forward to when you go to worship, how many of the things you've listed would appear on a similar list if you were attending a town meeting, a sporting event, a service club, or a party? Many of the social benefits of "getting together" in a variety of settings are the same. So what makes worship different?

Long ago Saint Augustine said that there is a longing in the human heart that only God can fill. Honoring that longing in the context of worship is the most important thing a worship leader can do. In worship, a setting is created where worshipers realize something eternal is happening, something unique and transformative is taking place. The normal activities we enjoy and the conversations we have with others are "caught up" in a cosmic dance wherein our deep longings and God's loving embrace meet. Attentive worship leaders know this dance could be *the* dance that recreates a life, transforms a relationship, fulfills a destiny, forges a future, heals a wound, lights a fire, or plants a seed.

Emily Dickinson once wrote, "Not knowing when the dawn will come, I open every door." As worship leaders, we don't know how someone's life will be transformed in worship or how God will choose to act, but we do know that God is waiting to do more than we can imagine. Because we believe God is constantly making things new, we open every door, offer many tools and resources, lead a variety of songs, move out of the limelight, and allow the congregation to do what they've come to do—give their lives to the Creator of the universe.

The Worship Team

> In the quantum world, relationships are not just interesting; to many physicists, they are all there is to reality.
> —Margaret Wheatley, *Leadership and the New Science*

Relationships are all there is to reality? In a society that regularly gathers at the shrine of individualism, that is a shocking statement. Yet the promise of grace-filled relationships is the essence of the gospel. It is within the church—that divine/human, mystical/organic, loving/contentious place—that we can practice the skills of intentional relationships. Furthermore, within the wider church family the sacred action of worship becomes a living experience wherein the real dramas of human life can find expression, healing, forgiveness, reconciliation, peace, and energy. All of this can find its voice through the gifts and opportunities of "team ministry."

The dictionary defines "team" as "a number of persons associated in a joint action or endeavor." This definition may describe the word, but it does not come close to describing its meaning. The reality of "team" is not to be found in classroom descriptions. The meaning of the word is discovered through shared experience. The *quality* of the association—and not the fact of the association—is what defines "team." Many people "associate together in a joint effort," but the association in itself does not equal "team."

On a recent visit to the historic Pennsylvania State House on Independence Mall in Philadelphia—in the room where the architects of a new government designed, forged, and finally signed a document that would unite diverse colonies into a new nation—an enthusiastic guide opened a door of insight. He reminded us that the most important ingredient in those two-hundred-plus-year-old deliberations was each participant's ability to compromise. "Everyone present," he said, "knew they had to give up something. No one could go back to their colonial constituencies having received everything they wanted." Those founders wanted to create a team, but the first ground rule established was a willingness to give themselves away to the group—to surrender themselves to a process.

As with those who founded a nation, those who are willing to become a worship team need to surrender, for the sake of the church, to God and to one another. The key ingredient in the process is a willingness of spirit.

In his book *Will and Spirit,* psychiatrist Gerald May offers a helpful distinction between the words "willingness" and "willfulness" and suggests a variety of ways these two concepts affect our lives and relationships. He asserts that willingness and willfulness become possibilities whenever we truly engage life. "Willingness," he writes, "notices this wonder and bows in some kind of reverence to it. Willfulness forgets it, ignores it, or at its worst, actively tries to destroy it."[2] He seems to be suggesting that being "full" of our own will causes us to need to control people and situations. On the other hand, being willing leads one to a desire to give oneself to the flow, to the mystery of what is.

In my attempt to understand what makes a team come to life, I have found "willingness" to be the key that unlocks the team's potential. Each member of the team must make a decision to let go of willfulness and to pursue a desire to become a willing participant in a process that is larger than the sum of the parts. May writes, "Whenever one mires down in the willful attempt to master life, the strongest feeling encountered is loneliness. It is impossible to be truly, intimately close to anything or anyone when one is either controlling or being controlled."[3] He observes, ". . . willingness implies a surrendering of one's self-separateness, an entering-into, an immersion in the deepest processes of life itself. . . . Willingness is saying yes to the mystery of being alive in each moment."[4]

Mature relationships respect the mystery of each participant as well as the mystery of the process itself. Whether or not we call these relationships and this process "teamwork" doesn't matter. Understanding the concept of a team is less important than experiencing the nature of a team. As Christians, we often find it hard to let go of our willful attempts to create a meaningful spiritual life and instead to become willing participants in the life of the Spirit.

So it is with worship. Jesus invites us to become willing participants in a life of worship.

Unlike traditional "worship committees" for which a monthly meeting finds everyone around a table focusing on a particular function of worship, a "worship team" has as its primary objective a deep connection to one another's lives. Rather than a committee meeting with reports about upcoming awards and a diminishing supply of Communion elements, worship teams share life with one another, then spend time sharing that community life with God in an act of worship.

Out of this "life together" comes the planning of Sunday worship. A worship team might have its meeting in the worship space—moving, praying, singing, and creating as they discuss the form and flow of worship. Made up of a variety of people, including preachers, artists, and musicians, the team designs a weekly experience of worship that reflects the real lives of the congregation they represent.

The Threefold Movement of Weekly Worship

A logical, intentional progression is inherent in any meaningful activity. Athletes, artists, writers, and musicians affirm the importance of a threefold pattern for any event, session, or rehearsal. First, preparation of muscles, materials, ideas, and technique is critical in order to have a productive or successful session. Second, focused and mindful participation allows us to be fully present in the event. And third, reflective evaluation and integration of the experience allow us to grow to the next step of our development.

Preparation is the first step in the journey of worship.

A wise person once said, "In order to finish, one must begin." Equally wise is the statement, "In order to begin well, one must prepare." Effective preparation for any experience heightens our expectations, gives us added strength for the journey, calms our minds, and creates a sense of anticipation. Inherent in any worship experience are the words of Jesus: "Behold, I stand at the door and knock." Preparation for worship helps us open inner doors that might otherwise remain closed.

Prepare to give.

Worship is a verb. It is our grateful and active response to the self-giving love of God in Jesus Christ. Giving our lives to our Creator as deeply, painfully, joyfully, and authentically as we can makes worship a personal and intimate encounter with the one who knew us before our birth and who calls us by name. Responding to that call with the gift of life is the heart of worship.

Gifts are reflections of our love for another. The deeper our love, the greater and more personal is our gift to others. In worship, we give God our most personal gifts—the experiences, fears, brokenness, successes, and failures of our lives. Otherwise, our worship is mere acting, playing the part of someone else. An authentic and honest encounter with God involves the thoughtful and generous gift of the real "stuff" of our lives. This kind of giving requires preparation.

Prepare to be thankful.

Scripture encourages us to cultivate grateful hearts by being thankful *in* all things. This is different from being thankful *for* all things. In worship, offering gratitude to God in the midst of life's complexities clears a grace-filled place within us where sorrow and joy can dance together.

Prepare to be honest.

In its most basic form, the word "honesty" means "truth telling." An honest person is sincere and does not lie. Based on the Latin roots *sin* (one) and *crescere* (to grow), the word "sincere" refers to a life that is genuine. The gift of our genuine self—with all its troubles, successes, failures, joys, and doubts—is the most precious gift we can give to God in worship.

> Going through the motions doesn't please you, a flawless performance is nothing to you. I learned God-worship when my pride was shattered. Heart-shattered lives ready for love don't for a moment escape God's notice. (Psalm 51:16-17, The Message)

Prepare to be real.

What is real? In her enduring book, *The Velveteen Rabbit*, Margery Williams gives us this well-known illustration:

> "What is REAL?" asked the Rabbit [to the Skin Horse] one day, when they were lying side by side near the nursery fender, before Nana came to tidy the room. "Does it mean having things that buzz inside you and a stick-out handle?"
>
> "Real isn't how you are made," said the Skin Horse. "It's a thing that happens to you. When a child loves you for a long, long time, not just to play with, but REALLY loves you, then you become Real."
>
> "Does it hurt?" asked the Rabbit.
>
> "Sometimes," said the Skin Horse, for he was always truthful. "When you are Real you don't mind being hurt."
>
> "Does it happen all at once, like being wound up," he asked, "or bit by bit?"
>
> "It doesn't happen all at once," said the Skin Horse. "You become. It takes a long time. That's why it doesn't happen often to people who break easily, or have sharp edges, or who have to be carefully kept. Generally, by the time you are Real, most of your hair has been loved off, and your eyes drop out and you get loose in the joints and very shabby. But these things don't matter at all, because once you are Real you can't be ugly, except to people who don't understand."
>
> "I suppose *you* are real?" said the Rabbit. And then he wished

he had not said it, for he thought the Skin Horse might be sensitive. But the Skin Horse only smiled.

"The Boy's Uncle made me Real," he said. "That was a great many years ago; but once you are Real you can't become unreal again. It lasts for always."

The Rabbit sighed. He thought it would be a long time before this magic called Real happened to him. He longed to become Real, to know what it felt like; and yet the idea of growing shabby and losing his eyes and whiskers was rather sad. He wished that he could become it without these uncomfortable things happening to him.[5]

If we affirm the wisdom of this story, becoming real is a process. Perhaps the New Testament word *telios* describes best this kind of "reality in process." The apostle Paul urges us to discern the will of God, that which is good, acceptable, and mature (*teleion*) (Romans 12:2, paraphrase). *Telios* suggests a growing up into that which we have been created to be. Like the rabbit, we often wish it could happen to us without discomfort. But the steps to maturity are necessarily immature. We aren't born mature adults, and we aren't reborn as mature Christians.

Being recreated in the likeness of Christ involves mistakes and missteps. Being real and becoming mature is a process of letting oneself be truly and deeply loved, truly and directly in contact with the divine, touched enough to have our hair worn off! It requires the willingness to reveal our mistakes and to allow ourselves to be loved through that very wound. As we bring the reality of our mistakes and missteps to God in worship, seeking forgiveness on the altar of God's mercy and grace, the transformation of our hearts over time will bear fruit and bless those around us.

Prepare to risk.

> I firmly believe that travel ought to be a voyage of discovery rather than a ritual of reassurance.
>
> —William Ecenbarger

By its very nature, travel is beyond our control. Even in this age of high-tech communication, travelers often end up missing a connection and spending an unplanned night at an airport hotel. Journey involves risk.

Worship is a journey, an adventure into the mystery and majesty of God. Too often the journey of worship is designed to minimize risk. We come to the sanctuary with reassurance and comfort in mind. Our songs and prayers ring with hope and harmony. As we celebrate the immanent, heartfelt aspects of God, we feel safe and secure. This comforting dimension of worship is important and necessary. But are we as willing in worship to take the risk of discovery? To turn, as Moses did, to a flaming bush? To venture out into the wilderness because that's where the transcendent God, the pillar of fire, is leading us? As worship leaders, are we willing to guide worshipers into an unknown land? As worshipers, how often do we go there ourselves?

Prepare to be vulnerable.

The word "vulnerable" comes from the Latin word *vulnera*, meaning "wound." Vulnerability in worship implies a willingness to open our wounds to God. In the artwork of many "indigenous" artists, a flaw is purposefully drawn, crafted, or woven into the design as a symbol of that place where "the Spirit gets in." Our inner wounds may seem like defects or flaws but may become the very chink in our armor where God's love can touch us most deeply. Are you willing to let God enter through your wounds? Are you prepared to offer those wounds to God in worship?

Prepare to receive.

> "A sower went out to sow his seed; and as he sowed, some fell on the path and was trampled on, and the birds of the air ate it up. Some fell on the rock; and as it grew up, it withered for lack of moisture. Some fell among thorns, and the thorns grew with it and choked it. Some fell into good soil, and when it grew, it produced a hundredfold." As he said this, he called out, "Let anyone with ears to hear listen!" (Luke 8:5–8, NRSV)

In the parable of the sower, Jesus describes four kinds of soil: compacted soil, rocky soil, overgrown soil, and good soil. These words of Jesus help us understand the importance of preparation if we expect the seed to take root. In this story, the seed of God's Word took root only in the soil that was prepared and ready.

Farmers tell us a bountiful crop lies in the quality and readiness of the soil. In order for a seed to sprout and take root, the place where the seed is planted must be fertile and ready to receive the seed. Only then can the seed find the nourishment it needs to take root. But one does not need to be a farmer to know this truth. Anyone who has ever planted a garden knows the importance of preparation in making soil ready for planting.

The heart of a worshiper can be seen as soil. In fact, the very root of the word "human" means "fertile soil." To be fully human in worship means to have a ready and fertile heart, prepared to receive the life-giving seeds God wants to plant in us.

What is involved in preparation? All soil needs to be cultivated. Hard soil needs to be softened, prickly soil needs to be cleaned, and rocky soil needs to be cleared. Each of these aspects of preparation takes time.

In our world, time is an important commodity. Time has become something precious that belongs to us, and *we* decide how to "spend" it. In order to prepare a worshiping heart each week, rather than spending time, we need to *invest* it. Invest your time in preparation for worship.

Prepare to listen.

God speaks in a variety of ways, at surprising times, and through unexpected experiences. The word "obedience" comes from the Latin word *audere*, meaning "to listen." One who is obedient to God is one who has learned to listen deeply to God's voice. Worship provides the time, space, and place to practice the sacred act of listening. Come to worship with open ears, eyes, and hearts.

Prepare to be surprised.

Prayer takes us by surprise. It sets the heart free and releases a surge of new life.

—Brother Roger of Taizé

sur•prise:

1. to encounter unexpectedly; to take or catch unawares
2. to cause to feel wonder, astonishment, or amazement

Have you ever been invited to a surprise party? Perhaps you've thrown a surprise party for someone else. There are two main ingredients in a good surprise: the one being surprised thinks that he or she was about to do something else, and the one creating the surprise is happy and pleased to provide an unexpected delight. In worship, we often plan the details, lock them into an order of service, and follow our plans to the letter. Then we stand at the door while people tell us what a good job we did. God, the one wanting to surprise us, is too often left out of the celebration. By its very nature, surprise is to be avoided by anyone wanting to stay the same. By the same definition, surprise is a welcome guest at the table of abundant living.

What would worship look like if we expected to be surprised? To be encountered by God in such a way that we feel wonder and amazement? To be caught by the Spirit unawares?

Plan moments in worship that are beyond your control. Allow a testimony or an unplanned song to bloom in the midst of your carefully planted worship fields. The blossoms will be a surprise to everyone present.

Prepare to change.

[God] was like an eagle hovering over its nest, overshadowing its young, then spreading its wings, lifting them into the air, teaching them to fly. (Deuteronomy 32:11-12, The Message)

In this beautiful image, the writer of Deuteronomy reassures us that God, like a mother eagle, hovers over us and keeps us safe. The passage also teaches us that mother eagles will not hover forever. An adult eagle knows that in order for a young eagle to become the elegant, graceful, grown-up bird it is meant to become, that youngster will have to leave the nest and learn to fly on its own.

Eagle experts tell us that adult eagles are constantly helping their young ones prepare for the changes that await them. The process begins gently, as the adult eagle tempts the young with food, causing the young to flap their wings and fly inside the nest. The coaxing becomes more and more extreme to the point that the adult eagles tear the nest apart, causing the young eagles to fall and eventually attempt flight. The animal kingdom seems to understand that change is part of the fabric of life. In worship, as we open ourselves to the inevitable changes that await us, God gives us wings, coaxes us to fly, and constantly nurtures us into the new creations we are becoming in Christ. Welcoming change will enable us to live fully.

Worship leader, prepare to lead.

Worship leaders must find ways to become lead worshipers. As a worship leader, you are in front of the congregation not to tell them what to do or to perform for them. You are there to invite them into the act of worship in which you are already participating.

Become a lead worshiper by recognizing and affirming the priority of worship in your own life. Do you value the opportunity to give your life to God in worship? Before the worship service begins, find the time and space to prepare for your own encounter with God.

Stop at the doorway to the sanctuary and say:

"O God, I calm my mind,
I open my heart.
Fully present to you,
I enter the mystery of who you are
And who you've created me to become."

Worship leader, prepare your congregation.

Help your congregation prepare for worship by developing a sense of anticipation that God will be present in worship, that God will speak to us in worship, and that listening to God's voice in worship will transform our lives.

Offer a weekly preparation gathering or gatherings. Make it a simple time of self-reflection with the reading of the Scripture text for the upcoming Sunday serving as the central focus. The following is a suggested format for leading such a gathering.

Arrange seating in a circle without tables. This open space promotes listening. Light a candle in the center of the circle to symbolize the living presence of Christ in your midst. The one lighting the candle might offer a sentence or two affirming Christ's presence within and among those gathered. Invite the group to hold five minutes of silence. Group silence creates spaciousness and provides a transition from the noise and busyness of life to the focused reflection of the group. In addition, silence places the group's attention on listening rather than talking.

Read the text aloud twice, asking each participant to be especially aware of a word or phrase that is particularly important or meaningful. Ask them to whisper that word or phrase slowly during a moment of silence. On your signal, invite them to say the word or phrase aloud and write it down.

Read the text aloud twice, asking participants to let the images or sensations prompted by the text sink deeply into their minds. In the silence, ask the questions, "What is God's message to you in this text?" "What does it mean in your life?" "What personal associations do you make as you listen?" Ask participants to make notes on what they've sensed or perceived.

Read the text aloud twice, asking participants to reflect on their response to the Scripture. In the silence, ask the questions, "What is God inviting you to do?" "How do these words or phrases lead you to action?" "What is one thing in your life that will be different because of these words or phrases?" Ask participants to make notes on what they've learned.

Close this time of listening with a prayer of thanksgiving, followed by a time of informal group interaction.

Experience is the second step in the journey of worship.

In worship, we gather to remember the mighty acts of God in history; to celebrate the life, death, and resurrection of Jesus; and to be empowered by the Holy Spirit for service in the world. One of the unexplored possibilities in many congregations is an intentional encounter with the living, triune God. The word "religion" implies reconnection. As our highest religious act, worship reconnects us with God and to one another. If the congregation had the best tools to help them worship, how would this help them to connect with God? What would this connection look and feel like?

The Great Commandment

In the Gospel of Mark, Jesus had a confrontation with a "teacher of the law" who asked him which commandment was the most important.

> "The most important one," answered Jesus, "is this: 'Hear, O Israel, the Lord our God, the Lord is one. Love the Lord your God with all your heart and with all your soul and with all your mind and with all your strength.' The second is this: 'Love your neighbor as yourself.' There is no commandment greater than these."
>
> —Mark 12:29-31, NIV

With these words, Jesus reminds us how to love God: with heart, mind, strength, and soul. He also tells us how to love others: "as yourself." These vertical and horizontal dimensions of love give us the crux or "cross" of Jesus' message. Loving God (vertical) and loving others (horizontal) are the top priorities for those who call themselves his disciples.

Jesus and modern brain research

According to a breakthrough in the 1960s in the understanding of brain biology by Dr. Paul MacLean at the National Institute for Mental Health, the threefold human capacity for love offered by Jesus in the great commandment—that of heart, mind, and strength—is a description of the natural division of the human brain. The fourth capacity of "soul" is realized when the other three are brought into balance. In other words, when we live and love with the energy and capacity of each center, we become a "big-souled" person.

The three centers of the brain are these: the "strength" or brain stem, the "heart" or limbic system, and the "mind" or neocortex. The brain stem, or instinctual-doing center, shared by all animal life forms, is the "fight or flight" brain. It controls our basic functions, including breathing and involuntary movement. It is the body center and experiences itself in the lower abdomen.

The limbic system, or relational-feeling center, is found between the brain stem and the neocortex. It is the brain shared by all mammals. This part of the brain allows us to connect with others through positive and negative feelings and perceives itself as being in the chest.

The third realm of the brain is the neocortex, or conceptual-thinking center. This is the aspect of the brain that humans share with all primates. This third part of the brain handles short-term memory, creates judgments, and develops abstract thinking. This part of the brain perceives itself as being in the head.

In addition to modern brain research, many contemporary illustrations affirm the ancient wisdom described by Jesus. One of the most obvious is *The Wizard of Oz*. The three characters who accompany Dorothy on her adventure to find the "great and powerful Oz" represent the three centers of the human brain. Her friends can be seen as aspects of her life that she is slowly discovering through a perilous journey (the journey of life). The aspect of self missing in the tin man is the heart, or "feeling" center; the aspect of self missing in the lion is the strength, or "doing" center; and the aspect of self missing in the scarecrow is the mind, or "thinking" center. When all three are realized, Dorothy goes "home."

Another contemporary illustration confirming the ancient wisdom of Jesus is a program called 4-H. Popular in agricultural communities, 4-H teaches young people four priorities in life—to live with Head (thinking center), Heart (feeling center), and Hands (doing center). When those three aspects of self are balanced, a young person has a credible claim on the fourth element, which is Health.

Jesus asks us to love God with our whole being. As worship leaders, how can we help the congregation do what Jesus asks of us? What would worship look like if we gave our congregations the resources they need to love God with all aspects of self—mind, heart, and strength? What would worship look like if we had a balance of thinking, feeling, and doing? How can we help participants think creatively, connect deeply, and move meaningfully as a total act of worship?

In worship, we have the opportunity to love God using the three-fold capacities described by Jesus in the Great Commandment. What would worship look like if we took Jesus seriously by helping our congregations love God in this multifaceted way?

Meaningful ritual

Cycles of renewal, rhythms of transition, and the ebb and flow of life are as old as the earth itself. The waxing and waning of the moon signal the turning of days and weeks into months as the seasons become a ritual of natural transition carrying us through the year. In ancient cultures, putting form to these natural transitions became a way for human beings to mark cycles of renewal, birth, growth, and death.

Practicing rituals requires courage, vision, humor, and creativity, as well as the belief that ritual allows us to awaken to something bigger than ourselves. By marking the transitions of life through meaningful ritual, worshipers tap into the mystery of God's grace across time and space.

More than a meaningless routine, ritual evokes mindful awareness from the inside out. On an individual basis, personal rituals coax meaning from our inner worlds. As a community, group ritual draws our common experiences into the light and allows the time necessary to discover meaning and purpose in our life together. Involving the congregation in movement, creative expression, and reenactment helps the community to experience and explore what is already taking place in our life together and to make contact with one another and with God.

In the 2000 Olympic Games in Sydney, Australia, a young American Greco-Roman wrestler named Rulan Gardner, in a surprising victory, won the gold medal by defeating Aleksander Karelin, who was a three-time gold medalist unbeaten in thirteen years. Four years later, after winning a bronze medal in Athens, Gardner retired from wrestling and left his wrestling shoes on the mat, which is the traditional way for wrestlers to signal their last match.

This simple and profound ritual allowed everyone watching to become involved and to experience the meaning of his transition. Following the medal ceremony, in front of thousands of spectators around the world, Gardner lumbered out to the center of the mat and quietly sat down. In the silence and reverence of that moment, as he reached down to untie his shoe, he was overcome with emotion and began to sob. Those in the stands and those watching at home could "feel" his transition and began to weep with him. After placing his shoes on the mat, he stood, turned his back on his shoes, and slowly walked away. It was a powerful, emotional moment in the history of Olympic sports. In that simple ritual of sitting and reaching for his shoelace, the meaning of Gardner's hard work and amazing career became real, not just to him but to thousands of people who shared the ritual with him. Head, heart, and body—thinking, feeling, and doing—came together to make that moment an unforgettable experience.

An Example of a Group Ritual: The Ebenezer Stone
Purpose:
1. To help participants let go of something in their lives that keeps them from becoming all God has created them to be.
2. To provide an exploration of a powerful biblical word and to allow the meaning of that word to come to life in an experiential way.

Props:
1. Blank strips of paper 1/4 inch wide and 8 inches long. (Use a paper shredder to make these strips from blank sheets of letter-size copy paper.)
2. Pie dishes or other shallow dishes at least 10 inches in diameter. Use one dish for every ten people present.
3. River rocks at least 1 1/2 inches in diameter. Have enough to fill each dish and for all participants to take one rock.
4. A pillar or taper candle in the center of each dish.
5. Cards with an explanation of the word "Ebenezer." Create one card for each person present with the following information:

Ebenezer
From two Hebrew words: 'eben ha'ezer

This word appears in 1 Samuel 7:12.
It means "the stone of help" and reminds us
of God's constant presence and help in our lives.

Take a stone as a reminder of God in your life.

6. Small tables, one for each "burning bowl."

Setup:
Place the small tables throughout the room with plenty of space for participants to gather around or line up at the tables. Place the pie dishes on the tables, place a candle in the center of each dish, and fill each dish with a shallow layer of stones and plenty of water. Place 10–15 clean stones outside the dish on the tabletop. Distribute the "Ebenezer cards" among the stones. As people enter, give each one a strip of paper. (These could be placed in each bulletin.)

Process:
At a designated point in the worship service, invite the congregation to participate in a ritual of "letting go," using these or similar words:
One of the great songs of our faith is the hymn "Come Thou Fount of Every Blessing." There is an unusual word in this hymn. At one point it became a popular man's name, and over the years we have lost its true meaning. The word is "Ebenezer." In addition to this hymn, the word is found in the Old Testament book of 1 Samuel. After a great victory of the Israelites over the Philistines, Scripture tells us, "Samuel took a stone and set it up between Mizpah and Shen. He named it Ebenezer, saying, 'Thus far has the LORD helped us'" (1 Samuel 7:12, NIV).
The word "Ebenezer" is actually two Hebrew words that, in English, have been combined into one. The two Hebrew words are 'eben and 'ezer, which in combination mean "stone of help." Samuel raised an altar of stone and used it to remind the people that God was their helper.

Throughout Scripture, stones are among the great symbols used to remind people of God's activity in their lives. In other words, stones are seen as the "keepers of memory." Think of the huge stones used to build Solomon's temple in Jerusalem. These stones are part of an important place of prayer called the Western or Wailing Wall. For centuries, God's people have come to those stones to pray and to cry out to God. If those stones could talk, think of the prayers they could recite. In fact, there is a modern custom of placing written prayers in the stones as a way of becoming part of the dialogue between God and God's people through the years. Stones help us remember that God is present and active in our lives.

The other important symbolic element in this ritual is water. Water is present throughout Scripture as a sign of God's grace, love, and life. The encounter between Jesus and the woman at the well (John 4) is an example of the important place of water in the ministry of Jesus.

Allow the stones to remind you of God's presence and constant help in your life, and let the water remind you that God is continually renewing our lives, recreating us in the character of Christ.

Invitation:
(Light all the candles in the bowls.) I light these candles as a reminder that the light of the risen Christ is present in our midst as we gather here today. Scripture tells us that "in Christ, we are new creations. Old things are passing away; behold, all things are becoming new" (2 Corinthians 5:17, paraphrase). Worship provides a setting where transformation and birthing can take place. New birth often includes some kind of death or letting go of something inside that has become a barrier between us and God, something that holds us back and keeps us small. What is it that holds you back from becoming all God has created you to be? What is God inviting you to surrender in this place today? Are you filled with fear, bound by guilt, overwhelmed and confused? Whatever is holding you back, are you willing to let it go today?

As that thing that is holding you back becomes clear to you, write it down on one end of that piece of paper, and as you feel ready, move to one of the burning bowls around the room. As you approach that bowl, be especially aware of the thing you've written down. As you put those words into the candle flame, whisper, "O God, I give you this _____. I place it in your loving hands. As I burn it here, give me the courage to let it go and never take it back."

Then allow your fingers to let it go into the water. As you give thanks to God for helping you let go, take a stone as a reminder that God is your Ebenezer, your stone of help. You may also take a card with the information about that word. Take the stone and the card with you, and put the stone on your desk at work or in your place of prayer at home. Let it remind you that God helped you this day and will continue to help you in the future.

Music:
As people begin moving to the bowls, play "Come Thou Fount of Every Blessing" on piano, guitar, or organ, humming the melody line. When the majority of participants have finished this process, begin to sing the hymn. For the verse that begins, "Here I raise my Ebenezer," ask everyone to raise their stones high above their heads as a sign that God is our helper in time of need. Projecting the words onto a screen in front allows participants to have their hands free from song sheets and hymnals.

Integration is the third step in the journey of worship.

At this step of integration, we answer the question, "So what?" It's not surprising that the word "integration" comes from the same root as the word "integrity." Worship has integrity when what we have done in the sanctuary has meaning in the world and makes a difference in the lives of others.

In the Gospels, Jesus makes it clear that worship is not an isolated event, separated from the world and its needs. Authentic, spirited worship will always connect us to real life in the world. The quality of worship Jesus talks about allows us to practice our love for God in ways that will make it possible for us to live lives of worship in the world.

Any musician who has spent hours practicing his or her instrument will tell you that practice never makes perfect. Practice only makes permanent. Musicians learn to practice the way they want the scale or the music to sound all the time. If they practice a scale poorly, it will sound poorly. If they practice the same scale with focus and attention, it will sound clear and pleasing. Musicians' fingers will play a piece the way they practice the piece. Practice makes permanent.

In the same way, we worship God the way we want to live for God in the world. Practicing a life of authentic worship leads to a worshiping life, filled with integrity, honesty, service, and joy.

As you leave worship, carry these questions on your lips: What will this encounter with the living God mean? As I move into the world to love and serve people on behalf of Christ, how have I become a new person? How can my relationship with God become practiced, practical, and incarnational? As God "put flesh" on love through the person of Jesus of Nazareth, how will that love become manifest in me as I become Jesus' hands and feet in today's world? The journey of worship is not complete without integration.

Notes

1. R. S. Thomas. From "The Bright Field," in *Collected Poems*. London: JM Dent, a division of the Orion Publishing Group, 2000.

2. Gerald G. May. *Will and Spirit*. San Francisco: HarperSanFrancisco, 1987, p. 6.

3. Ibid., p. 13.

4. Ibid., p. 6.

5. Margery Williams. *The Velveteen Rabbit: Or How Toys Become Real*. New York: Doubleday & Company, 1922, htp://digital.library.upenn.edu/women/williams/rabbit/rabbit.html. 11 April 2006.

PRAYERS AND BLESSINGS FOR WORSHIP

Opening

Either you will
go through this door
or you will not go through.

If you go through
there is always the risk
of remembering your name.

—Adrienne Rich, from "Prospective Immigrants
Please Note," *in Adrienne Rich's Poetry and
Prose: Poems, Prose, Reviews, and Criticism*

Worshipers are immigrants in a new land. Like immigrants who have come before, worshipers are at risk. The familiar landscapes of the past are replaced by new frontiers. As frightening as they seem, frontiers are the keepers of unexplored opportunity. As nomadic people, modern Christians are always being invited by God into new territory.

The opening moments of worship provide a doorway through which worshipers enter a new land. The invitation is to leave "chronos" time behind and to move into "kairos" time. *Chronos*, from which we get our English word "chronology," describes the linear moment-to-moment time of life, the step-by-step movement of the events in our day. In contrast, *kairos*, the word Jesus most often uses in Scripture to describe the time of his death and resurrection, describes the quality of time within our daily events. *Kairos* helps us to stay inside the experience, while *chronos* moves us on to the next experience.

Given the proper tools, participants find that the routinized, "ticking time" of daily life has been transfigured through worship into a rich, abundant, open-ended, eternal, purposeful time. As worshipers are intentionally guided through the worship portal from "out there" to "in here," a kind of Narnia effect is created wherein dreams, visions, honesty, and depth are the norm rather than the exception.

As a worship leader, focus your attention on the threshold quality of the opening moments of worship. *Liminus* is the Latin word for "doorway." Thresholds are "liminal," in-between places—places of leaving and entering. The opening moments of worship are liminal and should be treated with intention and care.

Ask yourself, What thresholds am I inviting the congregation to cross? Where have the people been? What have they been doing? What am I inviting them to do now? Where are we going, together, in worship? How might the congregation be invited to let go of the attachments that hold them back? How will they be invited to open up to the Spirit's presence in their midst? Rather than leaving life at the door, how can they be invited to give their lives to God as an act of worship?

Ask yourself further, What signposts can they expect to see along this roadway of worship? What liturgical maps do they need in order to navigate the journey to which we are inviting them?

Thresholds

Put a photo of an open doorway in each bulletin or on the screen or both. Invite the congregation to meditate on a question or two as they kneel, sit, stand, or lie on the floor in preparation for the call to worship.

Possible questions:
1. What door is God inviting you to open, close, or walk through?
2. What do you need to leave behind?
3. What do you need to carry with you?
4. What prayer is in your heart as you enter worship?
5. As you enter, what do you need from God?
6. As you enter, what does God need from you?

Prayer of Preparation
by Jill Kimberly Hartwell Geoffrion

(This prayer is to be used by those preparing to lead worship.)

Once again,
I close my eyes;
I open my heart.
I ask that my words
be expressions of your Beauty.
In Jesus' reflection. Amen.

Alive!
by Terry Falla

Alive!
We thank you, God,
whose finger touched our dust,
who gave us breath.

We thank you, God,
who gave us sight and sense
to see the flowers,
to hear the wind,
to feel the waters in our hand,

To sleep with the night
and wake with the sun,
to stand upon this earth,
to hear your voice,
to sing your praise.

Our hearts are stirred
with each new sight
and sound.

Like a stream,
The whole world
Pours into our lives,
And eyes, and hands,

And fills our souls
with the joy of gratitude
and living gladness.

We want to embrace
and experience and express
every good thing in your world.

God our life,
splash us with the colors
of your Spirit.

This Is the Place

by Alan Gaunt

This is the place
and this is the time:
here and now God waits
to break into our experience:

To change our minds,
to change our lives,
to change our ways;

To make us see the world
and the whole of life
in a new light;

To fill us with hope,
joy, and certainty
for the future.

This is the place,
as are all places;
this is the time,
as are all times.

O God of this place,
and every place,
God of this time,
and all time,
here and now,
we praise you.

Gathering Prayer
by Cynthia Cearley

Gracious God,

In the church, this sanctuary, this sacred place,

There is a chest—a chest that holds the promises of our lives,
our gifts, and the hope of this congregation.

There is a cross—a cross that teaches us that God meets us in
our struggle and sorrow—as well as in our joy and happiness.

There is a table—a table that stretches around the world,
a table that sustains and nourishes our spirits.

There is a cup—a cup that is lifted in love by one who lived
God's presence in the world and invited us to do the same.

There is a pulpit—a pulpit where words of God's love, purpose,
and challenge are brought to God's people.

There is a candle—a candle that burns with the light of Jesus'
spirit, undimmed by conflict, sadness, and fear.

There are pews [or chairs]—pews that long to be filled with faithful followers who are inspired by God's grace and love.

There are people—people who are seeking, with lives that ebb and flow with joy and sorrow, tears and smiles, fear and courage, hope and despair.

There are prayers—prayers that we clasp tightly in our hands and let go to the listening Spirit of God—prayers for healing, peace, compassion, and justice.

There is music—music that soars to the highest point of this cathedral of faith and to the depths of our spirits, bringing beauty and inspiration to our hearts.

There is forgiveness—forgiveness that flows from the heart of God freely to our lives and spirits.

There is friendship—friendship that encircles us when we are in need, friendship that comes as pure joy, friendship that calls forth the best of all of us.

There is love—love that, as Paul reminds us, binds all together and makes a difference in the world, a difference that needs to be made.

O God, thank you for all we find here, for all we give here, for all we are here, together as your people. Amen.

Call to Worship
by Heather A. Hood

We come to this place seeking something . . .
    something better than ourselves;
    something that gives life meaning;
    some relationship that reaches deep into our
        souls to fulfill us;
    maybe even something to which we cannot
        put a name.

But we come seeking . . .
and even more important, we are sought by one who gives us
worth and meaning and value and love.

So, today, let us enter into this time of worship with hearts and
minds that are open to the one who has laid down his life for us,
who stands at the throne of God in support of us, and who reigns
in power for us. Come, let us worship.

Invocation
by Elane O'Rourke

To you, our creator, our mother and father, beloved beginning
To you, our sustainer, our shepherd and guide, beloved embrace
To you, our redeemer, our teacher and savior, beloved path
To you, beloved God, we offer our devotion and our praise.
Amen.

Invocation
by Patricia Ciupek-Reed

Great Creator, you have blessed us by making yourself known
in the wonder of the world around us! In times and seasons, in
family and friends, even in birth and in death, we feel the rhythm
of your love surrounding us.

We give thanks for your boundless energy, flowing to and through us by the power of your Spirit. We give thanks for the creativity and courage that spring from your power at work within us.

Therefore, it is with confidence that we seek your presence for this hour of worship. Bring us home to your heart, O God, and fill us with new awareness of infinite care, coming forth from your Spirit. Through Jesus, we pray. Amen.

Litany of Beginning
by Linda Fischer

Reader: Good morning, God—here we are!

All: Ready for connection and challenge!

Reader: What's that—we can't start yet?

All: Our "church face" masks? You want them to come off?

Reader: With boldness, no fear now—we present ourselves
    to you.

All: Our anxious selves,
    Our lacking-confidence selves,
    Our sad and lonely selves,
    Our courageous selves,
    Our playful and adventuresome selves,
    Our openhearted selves.

    Take us, all that we are:
    Awake, hungry, and waiting to taste your Grace.
    Fill us, we pray!

Amen!

Litany of Gathering
by M. Ingrid Dvirnak

(This litany works well with people who are gathering for a conference, as well as for worship in a local church.)

Leader: Eternal and loving God, though gathered in your name, we still stand apart.

People: We come from many places:
with our own histories,
with our own names,
with our own memories.

Leader: To this moment we bring a mixture of feelings.

(Various groups may give the following responses. For example, right side, left side, worship team, choir, etc., or women, men, and youth, or other natural groupings.)

Group 1: Some of us come in anticipation, expecting to be stretched into new life.

Group 2: Some of us come seeking, hoping for fresh insight.

Group 3: Some of us come burdened, bearing the weight of loads best left behind.

Group 4: Some of us come lonely, feeling unacceptable to ourselves and to others.

Group 5: Some of us come ready to be challenged.

Group 6: Some of us come joyful, celebrating friendship renewed.

Group 7: Some of us come anxious, fearing the unfamiliar.

All: But we come to you, O God. Together, we come to you because you have called us together.

Invocation (to be read responsively)
by Krysia Bereday Burnham

O Lord, here I am:
Weary and hungry for healing.

O Lord, where are you?

O Lord, here we are:
Wondering, we look up, toward your voice.

O Lord, where are you?

O Lord, the earth groans for you.
Empty, aching, watchful, we come.

O Lord, we call You.

O child of God, here I am.
O child of God, where are you?

O child of God, here I will ever be.
Come into my house.

River Us, Lord
by Rita Berglund

Many Voices: River us, Lord,
One Voice: May our rigid bodies form to a new flow of
community.

Many Voices: River us, Lord,
One Voice: With the energy of the Holy Spirit to change the
landscape.

Many Voices: River us, Lord,
One Voice: With wild creativity to carve a sacred path of beauty.

Many Voices: River us, Lord,
One Voice: With the knowledge of mountains to move in your
steadfastness.

Many Voices: River us, Lord,
One Voice: With the faithful willingness to fall into the pool of
your presence.

Many Voices: River us, Lord,
One Voice: With the understanding of the darkness where seeds
germinate.

Many Voices: River us, Lord,
One Voice: With the generosity of the sky to empower us.

Many Voices: River us, Lord,
One Voice: In surrender to the gravity of your love.

Many Voices: River us, Lord,
One Voice: In surrender to the mystery of your wilderness.

Many Voices: River us, Lord,
One Voice: As a home that sustains and nurtures a diversity
of life.

Many Voices: River us, Lord!

Gathering Prayer
by Mona Bagasao

One: We gather today to offer praise to the great God whose
name is I AM.
All: We, whose name is MAYBE, whose hearts are afraid, whose
minds are uncertain,

One: We, who renounce God daily in subtle ways, then wonder
   how to reclaim God yet again, not remembering that God
   never renounces us and that one claim from God is all we
   need,
All: We, who like little children, would praise God perfectly.
One: We gather to thank,
All: To love,
One: To reclaim,
All: To worship. Let our hearts and minds be directed by the Spirit
   in praise to I AM.

An Opening Invocation with Bodies and Voices

by Rita Berglund

(Rehearse with three or more individuals who stand up front and help lead
along with the lead voice. Allow a generous meditative pause between each
movement in order to fully integrate the physical voice of each posture. Take
each piece slowly and with great intention. Give individuals permission to
adjust the movements to account for any pain or disabilities and to do what
works for each of them.)

Lead Voice: With hands raised high, we greet this day with three
   shouts of Alleluia.
Lots of Voices: Alleluia, Alleluia, Alleluia.

Lead Voice: With hands palm down, we let go of attachments that
   create suffering.

Lead Voice: With hands palm up, we practice the humbleness of
   receiving.

Lead Voice: With hands over our faces, we honor the Creator of
   all faces and all lives.

Lead Voice: With both hands on our bellies, we bring awareness to the breathing of the Holy Spirit.

Lead Voice: With hands on our hearts, we consciously open our deepest selves to transformation.

Lead Voice: With one foot in the air, we honor the Maker of dancers and dance, the movement in each of us between falling and stepping and standing.

Lead Voice: Now joining hands, we acknowledge our need for community and our responsibility in community.

Lead Voice: With arms bent and held up out to our sides and palms forward and shaking, we shimmer in applause of God's generous grace.

Lead Voice: Bowing forward, we salute the presence of Christ in each other.

Lead Voice: With arms outstretched like wings, we reach out to bless each other with Christ's unfathomable generosity, saying three times: Bless you!
Lots of Voices: Bless you! Bless you! Bless you!

Lead Voice: With bodies standing tall, we bring an awareness to the bridge we are between heaven and earth.

Lead Voice: With knees bent and bouncing, we ground ourselves in the awareness of love, love in thought, love in action, and love in emotion.

Lead Voice: And once again, with arms reaching up, we shout three Alleluias.
Lots of Voices: Alleluia, Alleluia, Alleluia.

Call to Worship

by Michael-Ray Mathews

(This was inspired by the Emmaus Road story from Luke 24:13-35, with emphasis on Jesus "opening the word." It was also inspired by "Ancient Words" by Michael W. Smith and "Ours the Journey" by Julian B. Rush.)

Voice 1: Words!
Voice 2: By them the universe was created: planets and moons, stars and sky, all living things, day and night.
People: We come today to worship and adore the Creator of this world and this day.

Voice 1: Ancient words!
Voice 2: Words spoken long ago. The Scriptures we hold as central to the practice of our faith.
People: We come today to open the ancient words that will give us strength for our journeys.

Voice 1: Logos!
Voice 2: The Word through whom God created everything. The light that shines in the darkness and will not be put out.
People: We come today to seek the Logos-Word of God revealed to us in Christ.

Voice 1: The Word!
Voice 2: Jesus Christ—the Bread of Life—known to us in brokenness. Through Christ, we celebrate One Bread and One Body.
People: We come in our brokenness to become one body in Christ.

Voice 1: Living Word!
Voice 2: The Word that opens our eyes to recognize the Spirit of Christ. The Word that makes friends of strangers on the journey. The Word that warms our hearts with the Good News and sends us rejoicing.

People: We come to be changed—healed, reconciled, and
revived—by the Living Word of God.

Voices 1 and 2: Come, friends. Let us go on a journey together.
Let us be changed by the Word in our midst today. Let us sing
and give praise to our God. And may the church
be resurrected again this day.

Fire Up!

by Rita Berglund

(Designed as a call and response, the community calls out, "Fire up!" in
response to an individual voice. The following liturgical movements could be
added on the words "Fire up!": (1) hands moving as if striking a flint or
match; (2) a movement of receiving with palms upward; (3) hands moving
above the top of the head symbolizing the gift of fire at Pentecost. Note:
Energy and volume are key ingredients in this kind of call and response.
Shouting is appropriate.)

Many Voices: Fire up!
One Voice: Fire of all beginnings.

Many Voices: Fire up!
One Voice: Fearless expression.

Many Voices: Fire up!
One Voice: Willingness to mature.

Many Voices: Fire up!
One Voice: Courage in our grief.

Many Voices: Fire up!
One Voice: Passion for justice.

Many Voices: Fire up!
One Voice: Respect for others.

Many Voices: Fire up!
One Voice: Generosity of heart.

Many Voices: Fire up!
One Voice: Plumes of faith.

Many Voices: Fire up!
One Voice: Prayers of honesty.

Many Voices: Fire up!
One Voice: Tongues of compassion.

Many Voices: Fire up!
One Voice: Hunger for aliveness.

Many Voices: Fire up!
One Voice: This community into large soulfulness.

Many Voices: Fire up!

Affirming God's Presence
adapted from the Iona Community by Brad Berglund

Leader: Maranatha! (sung)
All: Come, Lord Jesus (sung in response)

Leader: Maranatha! (sung)
All: Come, Lord Jesus (sung in response)

(Someone enters from the back carrying a lighted candle and places it on the altar or in the front of the room.)

Voice: In the beginning, when it was very dark, God said,
    "Let there be light."

Leader: Maranatha! (sung)
All: Come, Lord Jesus (sung in response)

Leader: Maranatha! (sung)
All: Come, Lord Jesus (sung in response)

(Someone enters from the back carrying an open Bible and places it on the altar or in the front of the room.)

Voice: In the beginning, when it was very quiet, the Word was with God.

Leader: Maranatha! (sung)
All: Come, Lord Jesus (sung in response)

Leader: Maranatha! (sung)
All: Come, Lord Jesus (sung in response)

(Someone enters from the back carrying a cross and places it on the altar or in the front of the room.)

Voice: When the time was right, God sent the Son.

Leader: Maranatha! (sung)
All: Come, Lord Jesus (sung in response)

Leader: Maranatha! (sung)
All: Come, Lord Jesus (sung in response)

(This litany could be followed by a prayer of invocation or the singing of a song or hymn focusing on God's creative power, Christ's coming into the world, or God's surprising entrances into our lives.)

Prayer of Illumination
by Kristen Preston

With a single voice we come before you, Almighty God, and humbly lay at your feet the desires of our hearts and the needs of our beings. As sisters and brothers in your family, we ask that your unifying presence descend upon us, removing the marks of distinction and difference, that we may be one in your worship and service. For the sorrowful, ailing, and dismayed, we ask that you impart joy, healing, and hope. For the bound, weak, and distraught, we ask that you enable freedom, strength, and peace. From your bountiful riches, we have assurance that you satisfy every desire and fulfill every need, according to your will. Amen.

Prayer of Cleansing
by Antonia L. Jones-Wynn

God of grace and God of glory, it is in you that we live and have life. When we are in your presence, we find joy, for we know that your Word is truth, your nature is compassion, and your Spirit is goodness. Please open our hearts and minds and cleanse our thoughts so that we may be filled with your Holy Spirit and magnify your holy name. Through Jesus Christ, our Lord. Amen.

O God, We Come (Invitation)
by Desmond Hoffmeister

O God, we come at your invitation because you said, "Ask and you shall receive, seek and you shall find, knock and the door shall be opened to you." We come calling your name because you promised that you hear us when you said, "Call unto me and I will answer you and show you mighty things." We come crying out because you told us, "I have seen your suffering, heard your cry, and I will deliver you." We come believing because you have always been faithful. We come trusting because you have always been truthful. We come hoping because you are eternal. In your name we pray. Amen.

Confessing

Theodore Wedel spoke of the Church as
the company of penitent and forgiven sinners.
Confession establishes our place in that company.

—William Sydnor in *More Than Words*

If we confess our sins, he who is faithful and
just will forgive us our sins and cleanse us from
all unrighteousness.

—1 John 1:9, NRSV

The word "confession" literally means "with acknowledgment." To acknowledge means to bring into the open, to put into words, and to make visible that which is hidden. Most of us would prefer to keep our passivity, our wrongdoings, and our evil, vengeful thoughts invisible. But like harmful bacteria lying dormant in our bodies, sin tucked away in our souls can make us sick. The first step in treating any illness is an accurate diagnosis. Once we name our sinfulness out loud, healing can begin.

Without confession, our power is lost and we become powerless to make genuine changes in our lives. Confession enables us to stop blaming others and to take complete responsibility for our own experience and the choices we make regarding how we live mentally, physically, and emotionally in the world. Taking responsibility for our own thoughts, feelings, and actions allows us to regain our own power to change.

Nowhere has this fact been more evident in the past decade than in South Africa. The Truth and Reconciliation Commission, set up by the Government of National Unity to help deal with the consequences of apartheid, provides a dramatic contemporary illustration of the power of confession. The commission began its work by disallowing blame through recognition that conflict during the apartheid period "resulted in violence and human rights abuses from all sides. No section of society escaped these abuses." During the reconciliation process, *all* sides and each person involved had to take responsibility for their own actions.

The constitution stated a need for understanding but not for vengeance, a need for reparation but not for retaliation, a need for *ubuntu* but not for victimization. (*Ubuntu* is an age-old African term for "humaneness"—for caring, sharing, and being in harmony with all of creation.) Bridges of reconciliation were built through the discipline of confession. Frederick Buechner has said that acknowledgment of our sin becomes a sort of bridge.

If you are in a church tradition that does not use a formal prayer book, your worship service may be missing this important ingredient of confession. If your prayer book includes a time of confession, the following litanies and prayers provide creative alternatives for both community and personal use.

Prayer of Confession
from The Book of Common Prayer, *"Enriching Our Worship"*

God of all mercy, we confess that we have sinned against you,
    opposing your will in our lives.
We have denied your goodness in each other, in ourselves,
    and in the world you have created.
We repent of the evil that enslaves us, the evil we have done,
    and the evil done on our behalf.
Forgive, restore, and strengthen us through our Savior, Jesus
    Christ,
That we may abide in your love and serve only your will. Amen.

Prayer of Confession
by Terry Falla

O God of life, we thank you
that in our work and our worship
your Son, Jesus, has been in our midst;
that your Holy Spirit has moved among us,
shaken our complacency, questioned our orthodoxy,
and challenged our conformity.

We confess there are many ways
in which we have failed to change,
ways in which selfishness still wins,
and divisions remain.

There are ways
in which our need for security
and longings for recognition
make us measure our lives
by the standard of the crowd,

Our achievements
by the size of our salary,
the location of our street,
the impressiveness of our house,
or the make of our car.

Nevertheless, you have called us
to adapt ourselves no longer
to the pattern of this world,
but to rise above the narrow confines
of race and culture, creed and color.

You have brought us together to be a new creation,
a community marked by love, and we thank you
for the ways in which this is true.

But never let us forget your words to us,
"I have chosen you to be with me,"
and that being with you does not mean
belonging to a closed or exclusive circle,
but rather following you into the world
to be your disciples, regardless of the consequences.

Keep us aware, O God,
that we can be the servant church
only as long as we allow you
to transform our lives.

Let our worship be an encounter with you,
and lead us to more awareness of each other,
our studies to new ways of expressing our faith,
our participation in your church and world
to relationships that last and allow others
to know you as their Lord.

And let our care for each other increase
until in reality it becomes the task
and concern of the whole church.

So that in hardship there is sharing,
in sickness there is support,
in grief there is comfort,
and in loneliness there is friendship.

O God, whose enduring love is our destiny,
we praise you that it is by your grace we
are called, and by your mercy we are sustained
so that we can follow you into the world
and can be the church by sharing
in your death and resurrection.

Amen.

Prayer of Confession
by Krysia Bereday Burnham

Though you show us the way
Sometimes we choose the detour
We'd rather walk through our own fire—
And learn from experience

Some of us have Bibles
Thicker than the rest
Yet they remain unopened
In the safety
Of our shrines

Some won't linger
Long enough to listen
We sit at a desk all week. We say
"Why Sunday too?"

Steer us straight
Open our book
Light our fire

As we offer up
Our scars, our infirmities
And check our earplugs and blinders
At the door
Leaving here
Our leftover news
Fresh-baked bigotries
And perceived wrongs

We unclench our fists
Drawing near to your Heat and Light
Open hands, unfolding hearts
Poised again
To stay awhile
In your holy place

Guided Prayer of Confession (incorporating silence)
by M. Ingrid Dvirnak

O God, in this maze of life, we often sit in a corner alone.
We become encased in ourselves, consuming our inner life
and becoming empty.

Forgive us.

(Pause for silent prayer.)

O God, in this maze of life, we sometimes run headlong in any
direction that seems to offer hope. We rush right by others in our
hurry to find our own path.

Forgive us.

(Pause for silent prayer.)

O God, in this maze of life, we have tried to hide from ourselves,
from others, and even from you. In our struggle to
just survive, we have strayed far from the fullness of life you
have promised us.

Forgive us.

(Pause for silent prayer.)

O God, guide us through this maze of life. Amen.

Prayer of Confession

by Bran Scott

Loving God of creation and salvation,
we are created in your image, full of infinite possibility
for good and evil, healing and hurting.
We confess that we have not always answered your call for justice,
for truth, for mercy, for love and kindness,
for respect of self and others.
We have not walked the paths you have shown us,
we have turned away from the struggle for life,
we have at times forgotten you.
O God of love and of caring,
we acknowledge our brokenness and our shortcomings.
We invite you into the root-bound places in our lives,
that our hearts might be open to healing and new growth.
Amen.

Prayer of Forgiveness

by Patricia L. Hunter

Holy and righteous God, with repentant hearts we come humbly
before you. We know we have fallen short of your expectations
of us. When we could have shared your love with a stranger,
we looked the other way. When we could have given out of our
abundance, we hoarded your gifts to us. When we could have
spoken a word for justice, we were silent. Have mercy on us,
O God. We confess our shortcomings and ask for another
opportunity to let our lights shine in a world desperate for hope.
We vow to live as witnesses to your grace and love. We will
live worthy of our calling and your promises. In Jesus' name
we pray. Amen.

A Confession for Women
by Patricia Ciupek-Reed

Leader: Loving and holy Lord, we enter your presence full of reverence and full of need. As we remember your goodness and recall your teaching, our shortcomings are brought to mind. Guide us, Lord Jesus, as we recognize and confess our sin. We have accepted the inadequacy attributed to us by others, denying the wholeness in which you have created us.

All: Forgive and strengthen us, O Lord.

Leader: We have hesitated in fear to embrace your gifts and calling.

All: Forgive us and fill us with courageous faith, O Lord.

Leader: We have neglected to speak out on behalf of one another, choosing instead the safety of silence and continued oppression.

All: Forgive us, and cause freedom to break through among us, O Lord. Fill us with your Holy Spirit, that we might be your daughters indeed. Amen.

A Confession for Women (to be read in unison)
by Phyllis Butt

Nurturing Mother God, we come before you as women who have—too often—believed we do not reflect the divine image.

We confess not pride but rather a failure to believe in ourselves as equal creations with our brothers.

We confess a modesty that kept us from living up to the potential you created in us.

We confess we have failed the girl children by not being models of woman as divine creation.

We confess we have withheld our unique gifts from the world because we listened to the voices—within and without—that told us that only certain of our gifts were of value.

We confess ignorance of you, Nurturing Mother God, despite your presence in the Scriptures and in our hearts.

We confess all these things and we ask your help in strengthening us to resist our oppression, because all your people must be whole in order for your world to be healed and whole.

We confess and we ask your guidance on the way to wholeness for ourselves, our sisters, and the entire world.

Litany of Confession
by Moon Louie

All: We come to you, our mighty God, and ask that you hear our pleas. We come with contrite hearts into your holy presence.

Voice 1: Who are we that we can come before you?

All: It is by your grace that we are accepted in your sight.

Voice 2: Forgive us for our frailties.

Voice 3: Forgive us for our stubborn ways.

All: Receive us back into your loving-kindness.

Voice 1: Take us back into your loving arms.

Voice 2: Let us leave your presence knowing of your forgiveness.

Voice 3: Let us live our lives as forgiven people.

All: *May what we do and say be pleasing in your sight, our God and Redeemer. Receive our prayer in Jesus' name. Amen.*

A Prayer of Confession (using the weaving/weaver motif)
by M. Ingrid Dvirnak

(This prayer of confession is written for two voices. It may also be used as a responsive reading with worship leader and congregation.)

Voice 1: Creator God and Master Designer, you created something out of nothing, gave us this world, and said, "Take care of it."

Voice 2: We confess our sins of weaving patterns of neglect, hatred, and destruction.

Voice 1: You gave us your Word, the Holy Bible, which gives us instructions for the patterns of life.

Voice 2: We confess we have often looked to other sources for our instructions.

Voice 1: Jesus, Master Teacher, you encouraged us to weave new patterns of living when you said, "Love one another as I have loved you" (John 15:12, NRSV).

Voice 2: We confess our reluctance to obey.

Voice 1: You provided a new design for humanity. You freed us to weave new patterns of ministry.

Voice 2: We praise you for those opportunities.

Voice 1: Holy Spirit, Breath of Newness, you empower us to be
ministers. Your presence is constant; your power unfailing.

Voice 2: We open ourselves to endless possibilities.

Voice 1: To weave new patterns is a challenge we can't ignore!
Guide our thoughts as we present ourselves to you during this
service of worship.

Voice 2: Empower us to respond in creative ways so the weaving
will continue.

Nine Prayers of Confession

These prayers are focused on nine compulsive ways that human
beings sabotage their own growth and development.

Number 1: Trying to Be Perfect through Attention to All the Details

by Deana Schneider

Confession:
Loving God,
 In my striving for perfection, I have failed.
 I've let the details of my life become my life.
 I've let my need to control others cripple my self-worth
  and theirs.
 And I've lost my way once again.

Words of Assurance:
My child,
 You have not failed.
 You've become distracted.
 Do not despair; remember who you are.
 You know the way home:
 Trust and patience.

Number 2: Searching for Love by Loving Too Much and Feeling Used
Anonymous

Confession:
Dear God, when I look inside at myself, which I really don't like doing, I find I think in a confused way, and I love others lavishly but with more need for reciprocation than I would like to admit. I give to others but often don't see others giving. I expect so much from life and from people, and when I don't get it, I want to lash out. Help me. I feel like I'm drowning in a sea of feelings.

Words of Assurance:
My dear loving friend, come to me first, love me first. I will show you how to love others. I will guide you in thinking through the consequences of your commitments. When you know my love for you and accept it into your heart, your problems will slowly disappear in a sea of gratitude.

Number 3: Hiding from the Vulnerability of Love through Accomplishment and Achievement
by Brad Berglund

Confession:
Almighty God, to you I lift up my life. Before you and these, my
  brothers and sisters in Christ, I confess that I have sinned.
Too often, I mistake how much I do for who I really am.
Too often, my accomplishments are part of an endless striving to
  prove my value and worth and to be recognized by others.
Too often, the image of success, competence, and confidence I
  project becomes a role I play, hiding my deep desire to be real
  and to be loved for who I am.
Too often, I am unable to release my desire for attention and
  admiration, too afraid others will see through my façade to
  a lonely, empty place inside.
O God, help me.

Words of Assurance:
Dear friend, you are forgiven and you are loved. My highest desire for you is to receive that love deeply into your heart of hearts. Let go of your striving, your need to impress others, and your constant activity. Feel your feelings, commit yourself to relationships that matter, and slow down so you can discover who you are as a human being created in my image. Use the gifts I have given you not for your own sake but to help others discover their true gifts. Step out of the limelight. Take the focus off yourself. Set others free to share the work to which you have *all* been called. And above all, put on love, my greatest gift to you.

Number 4: Taking Everything in Life Personally and Making It Heavier Than It Needs to Be
by Theodorre Donson

Confession:
Dear God, too often life feels like a jumble of emotions inside me. I become irritated at so many little things. I become fearful when people don't live up to their promises, which I depend on. I want to strike out, yet I know you don't want me to do that. You have asked me to love, and I do love them all. That's what makes the jumble impossible to manage. Then I sink to self-pity and envy others' lives. I don't know where to turn.

Words of Assurance:
My beloved child, life is messy, not as organized and predictable as you want it to be. In the confusion, look for me. I invite you to rest in my arms. Be comforted by my love for you. You are my child, my friend, my coworker. I care about you because you are my own. I will not fail you. I know you need my power and my joy, so I am giving them to you. I will always be with you.

Number 5: Hiding Oneself and One's Talents from the Community
by Karen Berry

Confession:
I confess to God, and to you, my sisters and brothers, that I have sinned through selfishness and greed, hoarding my time and space, refusing to share my thoughts and my resources. I have looked down on others, used sarcasm as a way of feeling superior, and remained uninvolved when there was a need for my participation. I ask God, and you, my community of believers, to forgive me and to help me to grow in transforming my weaknesses.

Words of Assurance:
My child, my mercy grants you forgiveness and challenges you to grow in selflessness. May your natural gifts of perception, humor, and knowing move you in the direction of sharing all that you are and all you have been given. And may compassion for those who need whatever you can give be the beauty that transforms your life.

Number 6: Allowing Constant Worry to Preoccupy One's Mind and Heart
by Susan Davis

Confession:
Most merciful God, I confess I have not trusted in you. I worry about every aspect of my life and the lives of my friends, my children, and my spouse. I am anxious about other people's values, their perception of me, and my great indecision in how to handle the events of my life. Most of the time, I am not even aware of this anxiety, except at the end of the day when my muscles ache from it all. I am so tired, Lord, of myself and my imagined scenarios. I am strangling. Save me, Lord, from myself.

Words of Assurance:
Precious child, I want you to breathe. Deeply. Move to that still place within, where only you and I reside. Look into my eyes and drink in peace and acceptance. This sacred space where our life is together is the single most important thing in your life. Come to it often. I am always here, waiting for you. Turn to me instead of to the many other voices clanging in your mind. Take time to grow this space with me, for it is only in my presence that you will find peace. Come to me, my precious child, and find rest in my loving arms.

Number 7: Seeking Self-gratification through an Excess of Consumption

by Robert Davis

Confession:
Most intimate Lover of my soul, only you know how much I struggle and search to find peace. I have forgotten who you made me to be and how you intended for me to be fulfilled. I have sought my own pleasure and not trusted in even the possibility of your divine inner peace. Give me your Holy Spirit and assure me of your presence.

Words of Assurance:
My beloved child, I intended for you to be fulfilled with the divine inner peace that I give to you, a peace that the world cannot give. I remain closer to you than your breath.

Number 8: Seeking Fulfillment through an Excess of Self-expression

by Joni Seivert

Confession:
O Jesus, help me to be more like you.
Let me release the need to think I know it all.
Humble me to remember that my purpose
is to be strong for others in a gentle and generous fashion.

Protect others from me when I get in my own way
by being bossy and overbearing.
Soften my words so others can know my sensitive heart.

Words of Assurance:
My child,
When you speak from your heart,
your vulnerable strength
shines through to light the way for others to follow.
May your passionate example be a
foundation that leads others to their innocence.

Number 9: Hiding Low Self-confidence Behind a Mask of Serenity

by Rita Berglund

Confession:
Here I am, once again avoiding conflict at all cost.
Drifting in neutral I withdraw to invisibility.
No voice, no life, I am safe, back in my self-imposed
    prison cocoon.
My knees buckle at the thought of really speaking my truth.
I cannot risk such rejection and abandonment.
I cannot risk finding out that no one really cares.
Peaceful and serene on the surface,
I project wisdom while hiding my inner despair.

Words of Assurance:
Come out of hiding, my precious child. I did not create
    you to leave you with no hope.
Trust in my presence, trust in my strength, trust in my
    unfailing love.
You are beloved and gifted with creativity.
Don't hide the face I have given you. Don't silence your voice.
Focus on the goals that empower you to hold your ground, and
    move with great intention toward your own transformation.

Lamenting

We live in a superficial, media-driven culture that often seems uncomfortable with true depths of feeling. Indeed, it seems as if our culture has become increasingly intolerant of that acute sorrow, that intense anguish and deep remorse which may be defined as grief. We want to medicate such sorrow away. But poets have always celebrated grief as one of the deepest human emotions. To grieve is to lament, to let sorrow inhabit one's very being.

—Edward Hirsch in *How to Read a Poem and Fall in Love with Poetry*

Grief is a universal human experience. Expressing grief in creative and helpful ways is less universal. It is an art form to be practiced. The poet Robert Frost suggested that poetry best expresses grief. He said that poetry must be free to "go its way in tears." When one thinks of poetic passages in the Bible, one is drawn immediately to the book of Psalms. Many psalms help us put our grief into words. Jesus, as a teacher in the Jewish tradition, knew the psalms of lament and would have put them to use in worship as well as in his personal spiritual disciplines.

Athanasius, a Christian leader of the fourth century, declared that the psalms have a unique place in the Bible because while most of Scripture speaks *to* us, the psalms speak *for* us. The Hebrew people of the first century made use of the psalms both in their liturgical practice and in their personal prayers. It is widely accepted that Jesus' words from the cross included the entire text of Psalm 22, which begins, "My God, my God, why have you forsaken me?" Filled with pain, Jesus allowed a psalm to express his grief by putting his anguish into words. Old Testament scholar Bernard Anderson identifies 47 psalms of individual lament and 14 psalms of community lament. Of the 150 psalms in our Psalter, 61 are expressions of lament.

It is often said that change is experienced as loss, and loss is experienced as grief. It is safe to say that modern Christians enter worship each week carrying some amount of grief. If we present ourselves to God honestly and authentically, our grief becomes an appropriate part of our gift of worship. The following resources are offered as tools to help your congregation bring that part of themselves—the deep, painful, grieving, brokenhearted part—into the light of God's loving embrace.

Psalms of Individual Lament

One example is Psalm 22 (NRSV):

My God, my God, why have you forsaken me?
  Why are you so far from helping me, from the words
    of my groaning?
O my God, I cry by day, but you do not answer;
  and by night, but find no rest.

Yet you are holy,
  enthroned on the praises of Israel.
In you our ancestors trusted;
  they trusted, and you delivered them.
To you they cried, and were saved;
  in you they trusted, and were not put to shame.

But I am a worm, and not human;
  scorned by others, and despised by the people.
All who see me mock at me;
  they make mouths at me, they shake their heads;
"Commit your cause to the LORD; let him deliver—
  let him rescue the one in whom he delights!"

Yet it was you who took me from the womb;
    you kept me safe on my mother's breast.
On you I was cast from my birth,
    and since my mother bore me you have been my God.
Do not be far from me,
    for trouble is near
    and there is no one to help.

Many bulls encircle me,
    strong bulls of Bashan surround me;
they open wide their mouths at me,
    like a ravening and roaring lion.

I am poured out like water,
    and all my bones are out of joint;
my heart is like wax;
    it is melted within my breast;
my mouth is dried up like a potsherd,
    and my tongue sticks to my jaws;
    you lay me in the dust of death.

For dogs are all around me;
    a company of evildoers encircles me.
My hands and feet have shriveled;
I can count all my bones.
They stare and gloat over me;
they divide my clothes among themselves,
    and for my clothing they cast lots.

But you, O LORD, do not be far away!
    O my help, come quickly to my aid!
Deliver my soul from the sword,
    my life from the power of the dog!
    Save me from the mouth of the lion!

From the horns of the wild oxen you have rescued me.
I will tell of your name to my brothers and sisters;
    in the midst of the congregation I will praise you:
You who fear the LORD, praise him!
    All you offspring of Jacob, glorify him;
    stand in awe of him, all you offspring of Israel!
For he did not despise or abhor
    the affliction of the afflicted;
he did not hide his face from me,
    but heard when I cried to him.

From you comes my praise in the great congregation;
    my vows I will pay before those who fear him.
The poor shall eat and be satisfied;
    those who seek him shall praise the LORD.
    May your hearts live forever!

All the ends of the earth shall remember
    and turn to the LORD;
and all the families of the nations
    shall worship before him.
For dominion belongs to the LORD,
    and he rules over the nations.

To him, indeed, shall all who sleep in the earth bow down;
    before him shall bow all who go down to the dust,
    and I shall live for him.
Posterity will serve him;
    future generations will be told about the Lord,
and proclaim his deliverance to a people yet unborn,
    saying that he has done it.

Other psalms of individual lament: 3, 4, 5, 6, 7, 9, 10, 13, 14, 17, 25, 26, 27:7-14, 28, 31, 38, 39, 40:12-17, 41, 42, 43, 51, 52, 53, 54, 55, 56, 57, 61, 64, 69, 70, 71, 77, 86, 88, 102, 109, 120, 130, 139, 140, 141, 142, and 143

Psalms of Community Lament

One example is Psalm 123 (NRSV):

To you I lift up my eyes,
    O you who are enthroned in the heavens!
As the eyes of servants
    look to the hand of their master,
as the eyes of a maid
    to the hand of her mistress,
so our eyes look to the LORD our God,
    until he has mercy upon us.

Have mercy upon us, O LORD, have mercy upon us,
    for we have had more than enough of contempt.
Our soul has had more than its fill
    of the scorn of those who are at ease,
    of the contempt of the proud.

Other psalms of community lament: 12, 44, 58, 60, 74, 79, 80, 83, 85, 90, 123, 126, 129, and 137

A Litany of Lament
by Rita Berglund

All: Come and save us!

One: The ground cries out with the voices of hunger. The rain flows with our tears. The wind of shame turns away our faces, and we are bent over by the greatest of sorrows. Loneliness grabs at our bones, despair turns our stomachs into stone, and the smallness of our minds drives us to fear and rage.

All: Come and save us!

One: Call us out of our forgetfulness, God. Awaken us to your steadfast presence. May we know you are not done changing us, not done carving out new possibilities for being with what is, for walking into that which we see as impossible.

All: Come and save us!

One: So that our hunger leads us to surrender to your mystery, to let go of our small view, to accept with open hearts all that is impermanent. We are shattered like panes of colored glass. Come and regather us, regather us into a new window, a new pattern of perception and beauty.

All: Come and save us!

One: So that deep from the ashes of our deaths will grow new life and new possibilities. Friend in our suffering, save us from ourselves. Save us for yourself.

All: Come and save us!

(The congregation might respond by singing "He Will Come and Save You" by Bob Fitts and Gary Sadler.)

Lament for a World in Chaos
by Linda Fischer

God, we languish in our misery.
Our hearts are heavy with sadness.
Our self-centeredness has led us to strife.
We are terrified of war as we recognize how ready is
    our tendency to see the other as "different, less than."
    We recognize our own anger.
Nature roars around us in places far and near,
    shattering what we know, as lives are uprooted.
    We cry and feel forsaken by you.

Sons, daughters, mothers, and fathers go without
    food and even shelter,
    and we ache for them.
Yet even those of us who "have" are doubtful of "enough."
    And we feel ashamed.
Sickness and infirmity come,
    unfairly advancing on the young among us and
    steadily announcing strength as we age.
    We are afraid.
This is all too much—we are overwhelmed.
Our hearts reach out to you—do you hear?

Yet as we suffer, we longingly hope.
And as we long, you are here.
You remind us of the "more" we find in you.
    We remember how you sustain, comfort, and encourage us.
We remember that your presence becomes strong in the world as
    we become your eyes, ears, hands. We take courage to feel the
    fullness of you in us as we make a difference by being who we
    are, your image-bearers to a world hungry for love. And we
    give thanks. Amen.

In Time of Grief

from the Salisbury Cathedral, attributed to Bede Griffiths

Lord Christ, life is eternal, and love is immortal, and death is only
    a horizon, and a horizon is nothing save the limit of our sight.
Lift us up, strong Son of God, and we may see further.
Cleanse our eyes, that we may see more clearly.
Draw us closer to yourself, that we may know ourselves to be
    nearer to our loved ones who are with you.

Prayer in a Time of Tragedy and Loss

by Linda Fischer

(This prayer can easily be done in the plural with "we/us.")

O God, I cry out to you!
My grief runs so deep I feel wounded and bleeding.
I never expected life to bring this—
this senseless illness,
    this mistaken judgment,
        this divorce,
            this accident of grave consequence,
              this painful death.
I stomp my feet and rage.
I feel hateful—where is my control?
How unjust! Where are you?
How could you allow this to happen?
I'm wallowing in self-pity and sorrow
Like a little child not getting its way.
I feel my tantrum adding to the chaos around me.
I feel ashamed.
I can't even recognize myself. What's happening to me?

Restore peace in me.
Let me value these feelings—let me know that I am normal.
Let me know I seek protection and meaning—I need shelter.
Let me know I will survive this storm.
Let me trust your presence
    to give me faith to hold on,
    to take things a step at a time until you anchor me once again,
    to find myself, though life will never be the same again.
May I know you as the Great Enough,
    the Ever-Compassionate One.

Amen.

Prayers following Violence and Loss of Life
by Rebecca Gale

Love Everlasting, we fall on our knees. Sometimes we are overwhelmed by the weight of the world and the incredible circumstances under which you ask us only to clear our hearts of the dark fear that threatens to overcome. In you, let us find strength to return again and again to silence, where we release into grace.

Lord, hear our prayer.

Tonight we mourn the loss of _____. And we offer our thanks for _____'s life. *(Invite others to offer words of thanks and celebration for the person's gifts and blessings to the community and to the world.)*

Lord, hear our prayer.

Tonight we mourn the terror and uncertainty that fill a being so deeply and transform to acts of violence. For those who sit in prison, for those who contemplate and carry out "the unthinkable"—but, Lord, this is *us*. How can we hope for a brighter day until we understand that every human heart, including this one, carries the capacity to hate and to hurt? Shower us with compassion, Lord, for we *all* are broken.

Lord, hear our prayer.

We pray for healing. We know it is ours—the hope, the joy, the unending love that radiate from every soul—*every soul*—and it is for this that we gather here. Let us have the courage of Christ to offer our gifts, to shine in the light, to use our power and our wisdom and our desire to fly to face and heal our pain, to open ourselves to purity of heart in Love's fire.

Lord, hear our prayer.

With the children, the homeless, the soldiers, the leaders, the downtrodden, the suffering, and the wretched, we all share a common heart. Gather us in your love, precious Lord, and hold us as we move in darkness and light.

Lord, hear our prayer.

Litany following a Community Tragedy
by Sally M. Brower

(This litany is a prayer for deliverance after an act of violence, negligence, or irresponsibility. Violence may be viewed as intended loss and suffering, such as a school shooting. Negligence refers to loss and suffering that were not intended but are the by-product of a decision, such as a corporation's ignoring safety standards. Irresponsibility refers to a momentary decision by an individual that results in loss and suffering, such as driving while intoxicated.)

Leader: A deep wound in our community lies raw before our eyes, burning a hole into our hearts. It gapes open like a giant sinkhole that cannot be filled. We can only stand at the edge and try to grasp the enormity of what we have lost, the lives swallowed by the darkness. We cry out to the Lord in our distress.

All: Hear our cry for help, O God.

Leader: Disaster sits upon our doorsteps, and fear is waiting, crouched behind each door. We shout aloud, "Why, Lord?" We whisper to each other, "How?" and "How could this be?" No answer can touch the dread that burrows deep.

All: Hear our cry for help, O God.

Leader: We must confess, O God, our first thought was not for others. Our shared reaction, our first and only prayer, was for ourselves: "Lord, let it not be my child." "Dear God, please, not my spouse."

All: Hear our cry for help, O God.

Leader: We could not stop ourselves from morbid curiosity. We slow our cars to look, ask neighbors for details. From a distance, we inspect the ruins, view the destruction, behold the broken pieces that shatter our illusions of safety.

All: Hear our cry for help, O God.

Leader: O God, we are scared and numb and beyond the help of human comfort. Listen to the cries of your people as you did of old. Look down on us in our distress and show us pity.

All: Hear us, O God.

Leader: Answer us, O God most merciful.

All: Have mercy, O God.

Leader: Help us to show your mercy. Move us to compassion. Free us from the fear that holds us back.

All: Free us, O God.

Leader: Let us not care for our lives only. Make us feel the truth that we are one people.

All: Their children are as our children.

Leader: Give us hearts to harbor those who grieve, hands to help where there is need.

All: Their flesh is as our flesh.

Leader: Incarnate One, you know our flesh, you feel our pain.

All: We are your children. We share your flesh and blood.

Leader: Hear the cries of your children, O God.

All: Abba! Father! Hear us.

Leader: The God of creation calls to us, "Fear not, for I have redeemed you."

All: Abba! Father! Hear us.

Leader: The God who formed us speaks to us, "I have called you by name. You are mine."

All: Abba! Father! Hear us.

Leader: As we stand at the great abyss of darkness, God is with us. When fear threatens to overtake us, God will set it to flight. When we walk in the footsteps of those who live this tragedy, we shall be protected on every side.

All: Lord our God, we give you thanks.

Leader: We are precious in God's sight, and he loves us. Through all dangers, God is with us. Through all tragedies, God works to bring good for his children.

All: We give you thanks, O God.

Litany following a National Disaster
by Sally M. Brower

(This litany is a prayer for deliverance after an act of nature or an act of terrorism.)

Leader: O Lord, your people are suffering. In one terrible act, so many lives were lost, so many people are still searching for news of those they love. So many are waiting for help that comes too late or not at all.

All: How long, O Lord?

Leader: O Lord, your people feel forgotten. In the aftermath, there is no place where "normal" reigns. The images are seared forever on our mind's eye, the stain of helplessness forever on our hands.

All: How long, O Lord?

Leader: O Lord, your people feel abandoned. In trying to make sense of horror beyond words, they look for answers. In trying to comprehend terror beyond telling, they are met with the hollow sound of silence.

All: How long, O Lord?

Leader: We cry out to you, O Lord our God. We trust in you. You who have counted every hair on our heads and see each sparrow that falls, tell us how we should not fear. Assure us that our lives are in your hands.

All: Hear us, O Lord of life.

Leader: We turn to you, O God of our salvation. There is no helper but you. There is no other rescuer we can call.

All: Hear us, O Lord of life.

Leader: We search for you, O God of our redemption. There is no comfort without your presence. There is no healing without your touch.

All: Hear us, O Lord of life.

Leader: We listen for you, O gracious God. You who bring the dead to life and know our every need before we ask, answer us in our despair. You alone have the words of eternal life.

All: Answer us, O Holy One of God.

Leader: You are the Lord who is at work, unseen, doing more than we can ask or imagine. Keep us from pointing the finger of blame. Reknit us together in our common life.

All: Let us see your goodness, O Lord.

Leader: You are the God who calls us your people and showers us with your mercy. Keep us from surrendering to cynicism. Restore our hope.

All: Let us see your goodness, O Lord.

Leader: You are the God who makes water flow in the desert and living water spring up in the hearts of your followers. Refresh our joy in daily living.

All: Let us taste your goodness, O Lord.

Leader: You, O God, are the creator of all that lives and the sustainer of all that breathes. Replace our desire for vengeance with compassion.

All: Let us mirror your goodness, O Lord.

Leader: You, O Lord, are the strength of our bodies and the courage of our hearts. Resurrect our broken lives and renew our living.

All: Lord, you are our life. Live in us, and through us, and with us. Amen.

Healing and Reconciling

Miracles do not happen in contradiction of nature, but in contradiction of what we know about nature.

—Saint Augustine (AD 354–430)

"This is how everyone will recognize that you are my disciples—when they see the love you have for each other."

—Jesus, John 13:35, The Message

Love is from God; everyone who loves is born of God and knows God.

—1 John 4:7, NRSV

Love is the nature of God. If Jesus was the mirror of God on earth, it is clear that this radical or "rooted in the nature of God" love broke into human history when he walked among us. Scripture tells us that the love and compassion required to do the work of healing and reconciling are available to those who consider themselves Jesus' followers today.

Worship provides a setting where God's people can open themselves to that radical love and become agents of healing and reconciliation in a world torn by extremism and selfish ambition. Many of the resources here demand creative application and sensitivity. Great compassion is necessary when we help others open their wounds to the healing balm of God's love. Great courage is needed when we step onto that healing path ourselves. Above all, great perseverance is essential in the process of healing and reconciliation.

Litany for Refreshment and Restoration
by Sally M. Brower
A Reflection on John 4:7-15 and Isaiah 55:1-3a, 6

Leader: Lord, I hear your invitation. Come, you call me. Come. I see you sometimes at the edge of my crowded life, so close and yet so many times, most times, I am swept up in the press of things and thoughts, pushing me forward past the reach of your gaze and your touch.
All: Come, Lord Jesus.

Leader: I want to stop, to step away from all that pulls and prods me, to step toward you, catch your eye. If just one time I could look straight into your face, I would know your invitation is for me.
All: Come, Lord Jesus.

Leader: Sometimes, my thirst is all there is. It takes over my life as if it were a physical reality, my tongue stuck to the roof of my mouth, my lips cracked, the taste of life bitter.
All: Come, Lord Jesus.

Leader: A thirst throbs deep in the belly of my longing. All around me the world offers me water, but none of it is fit to drink. And if it were, I fear I could not pay the price. And if I cannot pay, then my soul may become so small and shriveled it cannot be revived.
All: Come, Lord Jesus.

Leader: In those times, I am driven to seek you. I no longer care how desperate I look, running through the streets, grabbing strangers by the shoulders to ask if they have seen you, calling for you loudly like a frightened child.
All: Come, Lord Jesus.

Leader: Yet you are always there. Like a merchant in the marketplace, you stand amid your stall of sweet salvations with open arms, calling to every passerby, "Come to me, come and eat!"
All: Come, Lord Jesus.

Leader: And I with hungry eyes survey the sacred stories, sacraments, and sanctity. I am ravenous for all I see—the soothing refuge of Sabbath rest, the promise of sins forgiven to set me free, the shining transformation of saving love.
All: Come, Lord Jesus.

Leader: You turn your full attention to me, and I cannot believe that you are talking to me. My life seems so unworthy beside your wondrous wares. And I am struck speechless at your outrageous offer: to give without cost, to provide without price. Nothing in my life is free. I have learned that even gifts have strings attached.
All: Come, Lord Jesus.

Leader: Who do you think you are to make me such an offer? Living water from which I will never thirst? Are you a mad man? Or, worse, a charlatan, preying on my ragged hopes and heart-worn needs?
All: Come, Lord Jesus.

Leader: But beggars cannot bargain. The promise that I would never thirst like this again has already opened me to receive whatever you have to give. One taste from the waters of your well fills me with the will to live.
All: Come, Lord Jesus.

Leader: Each time I return to your wellspring, I feel the stirring of life and wholeness. Deep within me, I begin to feel your love soaking into my soul. Each time I return to you, some long-buried part of me is unearthed and brought to light.
All: Come, Lord Jesus.

Leader: I want to cover it over again, put it down deep into the darkness of my forgetfulness. But I find that your life-giving water has already worn away the ugly husk. And curled inside, instead of the regret that I remember, I find a fresh green seed of gratitude, growing into grace.
All: Come, Lord Jesus.

Leader: Lord, I hear your invitation. Give me that life-giving water. Give me that water that I will never be thirsty again. I know you are the Holy One, sent by God.
All: Come, Lord Jesus.

Leader: You know everything I have ever done. You know everything that has been done to me. You redeem all I have been. You call forth all that I am yet to be. "Come," you call me. "Come, and you will have life. Come, it will cost you nothing. Come to me. Come."
All: Maranatha! Come, Lord Jesus.

Litany of Reconciliation
by Sally M. Brower

(For use on Martin Luther King Sunday or other occasions when diversity within a congregation or community is causing tension and strife. This litany of reconciliation is especially powerful if done responsively with diverse groups. An earlier version was used in an AME-Zion congregation with both African American and Caucasian participants.)

Leader: O God, you created all people in your image.

All: We thank you for the wonderful diversity of people you have taught us to call "neighbor."

Leader: Enrich our lives by ever-widening circles of fellowship and friendship.

All: Show us your presence in those who differ most from us.

Side 1: Remind us of those poor, imprisoned, or impoverished persons it would be easy for us to forget.

Side 2: Remind us of those of different races, ethnic groups, lifestyles, and cultures it would be easy for us to ignore.

Side 1: Give us hearts of hospitality, hands that welcome, and a ready spirit to include the stranger in our midst.

Side 2: Give us eyes blind to appearances, ears deaf to differences, and lips unafraid to speak against discrimination.

Leader: O God of all creation, you call us to share one world, live together in one nation, and become one people in your church.

Men: Help us to confront each other without bitterness.

Women: Help us to work together with respect.

Side 1: Make us quick to forgive and slow to remember wrongs.

Side 2: May we see Christ in all our enemies and serve Christ in all our foes.

Side 1: Take away the hatred that infects our hearts.

Side 2: Break down the walls that separate us.

Side 1: Remove the barriers that divide us.

Side 2: Heal our divisions.

Side 1: Lead us from prejudice to truth.

Side 2: Deliver us from paybacks and revenge.

Leader: Teach us to respect the dignity of every human being.

All: *Teach us to love others as you have loved us. Enable us to stand reconciled before you.*

Leader: For we who were far away from God have been brought close by the death of Christ.

Side 1: We who had no hope have been made God's chosen people.

Side 2: From every family, language, people, and nation God has called us.

Side 1: Christ himself has brought us peace, making us one people.

Side 2: Christ himself has broken down the dividing walls, making us one body.

All: *Preserve our unity, that all may be one as Christ and the Father are one.*

Side 1: Through faith, we have all become God's children.

Side 2: There is no difference between Jews and Gentiles.

Men: There is no difference between slaves and free persons.

Women: There is no difference between men and women.

All: We are all one in union with Jesus Christ.

Side 1: There is but one body; there is but one Spirit.

Side 2: There is one hope to which we are called.

Side 1: One Lord, one faith, one baptism.

Side 2: One God and Father of us all.

Leader: May the unity that has come as a gift to us be expressed in acts of love and loving words. May our unity be a sign to the world of God's great love for all people.

All: Alleluia. Amen. Alleluia.

Prayer for Healing
by John Pipe

Thank you, God, for your healing power. Thank you for physicians, nurses, therapists, and all those who help in the healing process of persons with disabilities so that they can live long and full lives with meaning and purpose. Thank you for those who offer a helping hand, a healing touch to those with chronic illnesses, those with incessant pain, those who depend on others for some of the basic necessities of life. In the name of Jesus, the healer of our bodies and souls, we pray. Amen.

Litany for Healing
by Krysia Bereday Burnham

Leader: To get around pain, we must seek to dive down in it. Although in the depths of hurt we reach the ocean floor of our loneliness, we can train our eyes to see the light that plays on the surface above us. There is a hand, and another, reaching toward us, through the depths, fishing us out of the dark underworld, where we were doomed to crawl on our bellies in a place of perpetual night.

(Ask the worshipers to place one hand on the shoulder of the person next to them.)

Leader: We must not bear our pain in isolation. The hand of our community—like the healing hand of God—touches our shoulders. Through these hands the electric shock of divine love is conducted, even now, in this place. Where is your pain?

All: *In our shoulders, tense and torn with all that rests upon them. In our necks, bent over from concentration, thought, and even weeping. In our brains, chests, torsos, and legs, inhabited by strangers called cancer, arthritis, or leukemia. In our muscles, bones, and skin, scarred, thinned, and flayed by AIDS, malaria, hunger, or violence. Yet we are not always passive recipients of our pain. At times, we are the cause of it: it festers in our minds and hearts, which suffer from real or perceived want.*

Leader: The earth, too, throbs in pain. We think now of Africa, Asia, Central America, the Middle East. The spark of fear and hatred soon bursts into the flame of war. The fire of the gods that forged us becomes the site of madness. The blood of Iraqi soldiers soaks the ancient earth but does not dim her memories . . . Basra . . . Falluja . . . Tikrit . . . Baghdad. The blood of American and British soldiers finds its reluctant rest in an exile grave, and everywhere a mother's cries sound the same. We do not have to journey far to find pain. It lives here at home, in lives of "too much" that's never enough. In a country where "too little" closes in like a sinking ceiling and a flooding floor. In this the land of plenty where lack lurks in the wings, we call upon the healing hands.

All: *Reach for us, O God, in our anguish. Bring us up out of the deluge, and place us on dry land. Cover us. Be the balm to our wounds of body, mind, and spirit. Meet us in our hunger and thirst, and give us food and drink at your table. Touch the parts of us that no one else can, the dark places where we confront the diseased parts of our deepest selves.*

*If we are sick, help us to inhabit the pain so that in moving
through it and living with and in it, we let go its hold on us.
For it is in our fear of pain that pain has its power. But you did
not give us a spirit of fear but of love, supernatural power, and
a sound mind. Help us to claim that truth this day, whatever
our pain as individuals, as a country, as a world.*

Amen.

Prayer for Healing from Sexual Abuse

by Krysia Bereday Burnham

In search of eyes
To see us
As subjects

In search of ears
To hear our desire
And the song
In our muted voices

In search of hands
To lift us up
Not to touch
Where no hands should go

In search of arms
To enfold us
Lightly if we need it
Tightly if we're ready

In search of minds
To know us
Even in our shame

In search of hearts
With enough give
To make us room

In search of God
Who found us
Long before the search began

Litany: We All Have Disabilities

by John Pipe

Leader: We are all disabled by sin and sickness, by despair and
sadness, by hate and prejudice.

All: Heal us of those disabilities, O God.

Leader: Some of us have physical and mental challenges that limit
us: we are blind, deaf, and unable to talk, to walk, to enjoy
simple pleasures.

All: Give us comfort, patience, and strength, O God.

Leader: Most of us have limitations that make us blind to
hurting people, whom we fail to see or understand or whom
we just ignore.

*All: Heal us of the blindness that keeps us from seeing poverty,
racism, and sexism.*

Leader: We are all disabled by sins that keep us from seeing our
own mistakes, shortcomings, anger, biases, and weaknesses.

*All: God, we come before you acknowledging our limitations
and asking for your grace and mercy. Help us to be open and
aware of others and to see ourselves for who we are and can
be through the power of your Holy Spirit.*

Ritual of Solidarity with the Suffering
by Rita Berglund

Part 1

(Instruct everyone upon entering to pick up one of the small stones available at the door in baskets and to place the stone on the main altar. After everyone is finished, a chorus of voices recites one voice after the other.)

Voice 1: We stand here today in solidarity with all the women in history who have been stoned to death.

Voice 2: We stand today with all who have been stoned to death by violent words and violent deeds.

Voice 3: We stand today with all who have been stoned to death by the silence of those who stood by and did and said nothing.

Voice 4: We stand today with all who have been stoned to death by poverty, hunger, and hopelessness.

Voice 5: We stand today with all who have been stoned to death by war, greed, exploitation, and lust.

Voice 6: We stand today with all who have been stoned to death by loneliness, despair, and loss.

Part 2

(Scatter red rose petals over the stones.)

Voice 1: We stand today in solidarity with all the survivors.

Voice 2: We stand today with the survivors who have struggled again and again to stand.

Voice 3: We stand today with the survivors who have been bought and sold and sold again.

Voice 4: We stand today with the survivors who are the mothers and fathers, sisters and brothers of the disappeared.

Voice 5: We stand today with the survivors who have run for freedom and with those who cannot run and with those who are too scared to run.

Voice 6: We stand today with the survivors who fight against despair, hopelessness, and loss.

Part 3

(Among the roses and stones, place small candles and light them carefully.)

All: We come because it is all about love. A love that is deeper, wider, and stronger than all the world's pain. We come because there is a teacher who tells us that wisdom and true love can provide healing in the deepest, darkest, and cruelest of places. We come because it is all about love.

Celebrating the Congregation

The church is like the Incarnation itself, a shaky proposition. It is a human institution, full of ordinary people, sinners like me, who say and do cruel, stupid things. But it is also a divinely inspired institution, full of good purpose, which partakes of a unity far greater than the sum of its parts. That is why it is called the body of Christ.

—Kathleen Norris in *Amazing Grace*

The New Testament offers many images to describe the church. Two of those images—the "family of God" and the "body of Christ"—make it clear that Christian spirituality, by design, is to be lived out within the nitty-gritty arena of community. When the congregation gathers in Jesus' name, the scattered, "dis-membered" body of Christ unites, once again, to *re*-member Christ. Each week individual members actively bring the body back to life. The following worship resources focus on the life and work of the congregation, thus allowing those individual members to connect in meaningful ways with one another and with God.

Prayer for the Anniversary Celebration for a Congregation
by Cindy Bates

Gracious God, we give you thanks for this day, for the opportunity to be in this place and worship you. Life is so full— full of people and places and schedules and things to do. It seems at times that we are all moving, and yet we are not always sure of the direction. O God, be our compass. Help us to see when life gets filled with things rather than relationships, when life is a series of deadlines rather than daily opportunities to learn and grow. Help us to see your world as a place where we can enjoy and nurture your gift of creation rather than fight over who has the right to use it up.

O God, give us the insight and sensitivity to recall those moments when you have led us in the past. Help us to trust that leading and be grateful. Help us to believe you really do care about us, not only as congregations and communities, but as individuals. You know us, God. Help us to know ourselves. And may that knowledge lead us to more understanding, more compassion, more forgiveness, more love, for others and for ourselves.

On this day, we give great thanks for the way you have worked in the lives of individuals and families and congregations to grow and build this church. In many ways, the years have been but a dream. The time has gone quickly. Many lives have moved in and out. Many souls have been shaped and changed. Many dreams have been realized.

O God, we are grateful! May we live our thanks to you. Continue to be our wisdom and our light. Continue to be our "yes" and our "no." Continue to be the one who helps us to dream. On this day we give thanks for all those who have gone before us, making a path where our feet could find the way.

Litany for All God's Family

by Kerry Greenhill

Leader: We come from many families—many different backgrounds, many different experiences of mothers and fathers, sisters and brothers, aunts and uncles, children, grandparents, stepfamilies, coparenting, extended families, adoption and guardianship, and families of choice.

People: We give thanks to God for all who have been family to us.

Leader: We come today with wounds unhealed, wrongs unforgiven, abuse or neglect unforgotten. Family has not always been a safe or supportive place, and we struggle to overcome old patterns and generational cycles.

People: We come seeking hope, healing, forgiveness, and reconciliation for ourselves and our families.

Leader: We are gathered here as individuals with different gifts and graces, different callings and cultures, as people of different ages and ethnicities, different political and theological perspectives, following different paths at different paces.

People: We give thanks for the diversity within God's family and for the love and acceptance God extends to all of us as adopted children.

Leader: Let us open ourselves to seeing our sisters and brothers in all people, for we all share the same loving Parent. Let us learn to see all children as our children and to care and provide for them as best we can, for all the people of earth are part of God's family.

People: Let us follow Jesus, our brother, in extending the circle of care to all whom we encounter. May our God-centered lives bear witness to the God who is Mother and Father to us all.

Leader: May God help us here in this congregation to grow together, individually and collectively, to become a more loving and healthy family, in which we celebrate diversity, nurture wholeness, comfort the afflicted, and watch over one another in love.

People: We are God's family. Let us give God thanks and praise.

Guided Prayer for a Congregational Meeting
by Cindy Bates

O God, life is good. Life is filled with abundance! We pause this day to give thanks for the wealth of good gifts we receive from you each day.

Silent prayer

O God, life is also filled with challenges and uncertainties. We want to face our challenges and uncertainties faithfully and courageously. We pause today to lay before you all those things in life that cause us to fear.

Silent prayer

O God, your creation is vast, but sometimes our world gets very small. This day we pause to pray for your world, especially for those persons and places and circumstances where the need for peace and healing is crying out for your love, your hope.

Silent prayer

O God, your church is our spiritual home, but we also know our home is not perfect. Your church struggles within and without. For this congregation in your church, we bring to you those concerns and cares that affect our shared ministry.

Silent prayer

O God, life is filled with possibility. We confess that sometimes we do not see your vision or hear your call and we are often unwilling to be open to your guidance. As we gather today, may we see and hear. In these moments, we pray for your Holy Spirit to dance among us and lead us in the way. We pray to experience your presence.

Silent prayer

O God, we are thankful that you have called us to live in community. Draw us together that we might be a positive, powerful influence for change and transformation in the hearts and minds of all who are touched by this congregation. We give you thanks for one another. May our words and decisions reflect your presence in this place. In Christ we pray. Amen.

Celebrating the Family

The family needs to know itself as a people deeply blessed and deeply broken, a people who must celebrate the gift of life itself and the gift that is each individual life. The family is called to care for and empower each of its members, not simply for the sake of individual self-actualization, but also for the sake of the whole Church and all of God's creation.

—Wendy Wright in *Sacred Dwelling*

The resources in this section assume a wide definition of "family." One resource may fit perfectly in your situation, while another may seem out of place. In a few months, the resource that didn't seem to fit may be the right choice. The diversity of family reality gives us great cause for celebration while setting before us a challenge in ministry. Rather than a prescriptive set of rites and rubrics, these resources are designed to celebrate the many ways our commitments of love find expression and life in the wider family of the church.

Litany for a Newborn Child
by Albirda Rose-Eberhardt

The gift of life is one the Lord alone gives.

We praise you, O God, for the gift of life.

The gift of life is one we must honor and nurture.

We praise you, O God, asking for the wisdom to fulfill our calling.

The gift of life flows from the love of God.

We praise you, O God, for your love.

The gift of life is a blessing from God.

We praise you for being the head of our lives.

Lord, we dedicate the life of this newborn child to you. We offer up our own lives that we might be empowered to fulfill your will for the direction of this child. Lord, we thank you for your presence in the life of this child, the parents, the family, the church, and the community.

Lord, be with this child and with us. Amen.

Prayer for the Adoption of a Child
by Anne D. Kear

Today, O God, we are thankful for new life that has come among us as the (name) family has gone to (country) and returned home to us with a new child.
   OR
Today, O God, we are thankful for new life that has come among us as the (name) family has welcomed a new child into their family.

We ask your blessing on (name of child), (son/daughter) of (parents' names), and (sister/brother) of (siblings' names). Be with this family as they all adjust to new relationships and new experiences.

You created us to be in families—families that come in all forms and expressions, families that are places of nurture, love, and affirmation. Guide and love (parents' names) as they rear (child's name). Be with (siblings' names) as they learn to know and love a new sibling who at times might have many needs.

Give us the wisdom, love, and faith to provide a spiritual home for (family's name) as together we grow in faith and love in Christ. In the name of Jesus Christ we pray. Amen.

For Family and Friends
from the Salisbury Cathedral

Loving Father, we thank you for the gift of human love and friendship. Bless those who are near and dear to us. Help us to love, to give, and to forgive, that we may draw ever nearer to one another and to you.

For Families
by Brad Berglund

For families living with space between them:
living miles apart,
seldom seeing each other,
struggling with emotional distance,
separation, and loss.

We pray for reconciliation,
for creative ways to heal and reconnect
with those who once loved each other.

May your love become real;
your grace lead to renewal;

your strength sustain them
through difficult times.

Lord, hear our prayer.

For Parents
by Charlotte Million

For parents as they age,
we pray for
courage to do the difficult work of
cleaning, sorting, simplifying,

and a calming peace to walk through
illness and loss of ability or memory,
moving into a season of life that can be
rich in wisdom and perspective.

Lord, hear our prayer.

For Mothers
by Charlotte Million

Thank you, Creator Spirit, for
nurturing a divine spark
for our mothers and for all
who engage in the acts of mothering,

for the blessing of nurturing love
at the beginning of a baby's life,

for the precious gift of caring
for our own mothers as they
approach their end of life.

Lord, hear our prayer.

For Fathers

by Charlotte Million

For those men, especially fathers,
who model your love,

for their patience, strength,
compassion, and playfulness.

Inspire us to tell those
who are like fathers to us
how grateful we are for the ways
they enrich our lives.

Lord, hear our prayer.

Unison Prayer Celebrating Family and Parenting

by Linda Fischer

(This prayer could be used at a baby dedication service.)

Heavenly Parent,
    How thankful we are that every human being is a precious
child of God. This day we celebrate the blessing these dear little
ones are—to their parents and families and to our world.
    Let us remember, whether we are biological parents or not,
that you give all of us many opportunities to be nurturers, to
bring your love to those around us.
    Renew our commitment to make a difference in the lives
of children: to help them make good choices and assume
responsibilities as they grow, to help them believe they matter
and have much to give, and, above all, to nurture deeply their
value and worth as persons.
    Let us be mindful that children observe what we do more than
they hear what we say. May we live in a way that we model your
loving-kindness.
    Amen.

Infant or Child Dedication Service
by Russell Rathbun

Voice 1: That God gives us children is a sign of God's love for us.

Voice 2: That God gives us children is a sign of God's faith in us.

Pastor (to the congregation): (father's name) and (mother's name) have come before this congregation to dedicate themselves to serving their child, (child's name), after the example of Jesus Christ and to acknowledge God's act of love in bringing (child's name) into their lives.

Pastor (to the parents): (father's name) and (mother's name), do you dedicate yourself to loving and serving (child's name) after the example of Jesus Christ?

Parents: "We do."

Pastor (to the congregation): This service of dedication can occur only within the context of a community. You are here today to be not spectators but participants.
We all need to be surrounded by a loving community.

(If possible, the congregation moves into one large or many radiating circles around the family.)

The Christian community is called to be present to help us raise our children.
I ask (name) and (name), godparents of (child's name), and (name any other family present), along with this community, to dedicate yourselves to the support and encouragement of (father's name) and (mother's name) and to dedicate yourselves to loving (child's name) after the example of Jesus Christ.
If this is your intention, answer, "We will."

Congregation and family: "We will."

Pastor: Jesus provides us with symbols and ritual to help us mark significant spiritual events by acting them out in a physical way. The most frequently practiced is Communion. In the Scriptures, however, the first Communion begins with a symbol and ritual of service.

Before he raised the cup and the bread, Jesus took a pitcher, a bowl, and a towel; kneeled before his disciples; and washed their feet, saying, "As I have served you, go and serve others."

Pastor (to the parents): I now ask you, (father's name) and (mother's name), as a symbol of your service in love for your child, to follow Christ's example by washing (child's name) feet.

(The pastor or godparents take the child from his or her parents and hold the child's feet over a water basin, while the parents wash the child's feet with water then dry them with a towel.)

(Following the washing of the child's feet, the pastor should ask the congregation to extend one or both palms in a gesture of blessing toward the family as the dedication prayer is offered.)

Pastor: Let us pray.

Lord God, Parent of us all, we thank you for the unfathomable love you have for all of your children.

Bless (father's name) and (mother's name); give them the wisdom, strength, and humility to fulfill the promise of dedication they have made today. Always remind them of your grace and love.

Bless (child's name) as she/he grows, always making her/him aware that she/he is your child. Allow her/him to see your love as it is made real through the words and actions of those who dedicate themselves today: her/his parents, grandparents, godparents, and this congregation.

Give us all the grace to fulfill this promise of dedication of our love through the service of (child's name) after the manner you showed us in the definitive act of service to your children through Jesus Christ. Amen.

Pastor (to the parents): (parents' names), (child's name) will not
remember what happened here today. Tell her/him often of
the commitments made and the love shared here today by you,
these family members, and this congregation. Go in peace.

House Blessing

by Russell Rathbun

(The service begins outside the front door of the dwelling.)

Let all who gather here prepare to join in the blessing of this home.

(name) and (name) have made a life together and found this
dwelling to make a home. They have invited all of you to fill it
with joy and love, laughter, and loud voices in hopes that this
party (gathering, service) will imbed its spirit in the walls and
floors of this house from the foundation to the roof.

They have asked that God's presence here be celebrated, and
God's blessing be added to our own.

Voice 1: God of mercy, let all who cross this threshold add their
gifts and graces to this home.

Voice 2: God of mercy, let all who cross this threshold receive
the peace and hospitality of those who dwell here.

Let us pray: Make this home a refuge and a safe haven; protect
it and its inhabitants from any harm, natural or unnatural,
the ravages of weather and time, and the cruel intentions of the
wicked and the desperate.

Fill it with your love; drive from it all evil thoughts, feelings,
and residual spirits from former residents and past activities.

Let all who enter proclaim, "Surely the Lord dwells in this place."

Amen.

(The pastor could sprinkle some water on the door or threshold as the following is being said.)

By the grace of the Lord Jesus Christ, the love of God, and the communion of the Holy Spirit, I bless this home at (give address or location) and bid you all enter.

(The pastor then opens the door, and all enter. Drinks may be passed out, and then the pastor and all in the party go from room to room, blessing the rooms with the following.)

Let us fill this (name of room) with all good cheer.

People: *Huzzah!*

(The pastor concludes the house blessing with the following prayer.)

Let us pray:
God of mercy, we thank you for the gracious gift that you have provided our friends—this new home. May your presence always dwell here, your hospitality always be shared here, and your peace always be felt here. Amen.

Responding

It's astonishing how much responsibility
we carry as weight, rather than getting
to the core and heart of the word, which
literally means "the ability to respond."

—David Whyte

Perhaps the most unexplored area of worship is "responding."
Within the customary worship hour or hour and fifteen minutes,
there simply isn't enough time to allow the congregation varied
opportunities to genuinely respond to God's voice and leading in
their lives. But if worship is essentially a verb—in other words, if
worship is the active offering of our lives to God—then "responding" needs to be the centerpiece of the service. Perhaps it is time to
reevaluate the number of announcements, the length of the sermon,
the number of awards given, and the nonparticipatory musical
offerings so that worshipers can be given more opportunities to do
the work of worship.

The following resources offer a variety of tools for congregational response. The key ingredient in this part of the service is time.
Participants need a spacious, expansive arena of possibility in which
to respond to their Creator.

A Prayer of Hope

by Alan Boezak

Eternal God, we thank you for the prophets,
for those voices of the night against
the forces of evil, injustice, and despair,
those voices of resonant hope that keep
reminding us that:

It is not true that this world and its peoples
are doomed to die and be lost.

It is not true that we must accept inhumanity
and discrimination, hunger and poverty,
death and destruction.

It is not true that violence and hatred should
have the last word and that war and ruin
have come to stay forever.

It is not true that we are simply victims
of the powers of evil who seek to rule the world.

It is not true that we have to wait for those
who are especially gifted, who are the prophets
of the time, before we can do anything.

It is not true that our dreams for the liberation
of humankind, for justice, for human dignity,
for peace, are not meant for this earth and for this history.

We thank you for these voices.

Amen.

A Challenge to Accompany Christ

by Brother Roger of Taizé

Christ Jesus, by your Spirit you come and
　　kindle a burning light in us.
We know well that it is not we who create this source of light,
but you, the Risen Lord.
To all of us, you give the one thing that matters
and which is hidden from our own eyes:
a peaceful trust in God
and also poverty in spirit,
so that, with a great thirst for the realities of God,
we may take the risk of letting you accompany us,
O Christ, and of accompanying, in our turn,
those whom you entrust to us.

Help Us, Lord

by Terry Falla

All goodness and truth are yours, O Lord.
May no evil estrange us from you,
nor error darken our vision
of your purpose.

*Help us to discern your justice
and to understand your will.*

In adversity and prosperity,
let the promise of your presence
put strength into our souls.

*Help us so to trust you
that we may not be afraid,
but may work with you
in the service of the world,
proving your love by our own,
through Jesus Christ our Lord.
Amen.*

A Promise
by Werner and Lotte Pelz

Jesus promises a new freedom
within a new commitment:
"This do and you shall live."
We test the promise by letting our lives
express the hope that it will be kept.

Prayer of Response
by Brother Roger of Taizé

O Lord Christ, help us this day and every day
to maintain ourselves in simplicity and in joy:
the joy of the merciful, the joy of genuine love,
the joy of all who hunger and thirst for justice.

Grant that, by renouncing henceforth
all thought of looking back,
and joyful with infinite gratitude,
we may never fear to precede the dawn,

To praise,
   to bless,
      and to sing
         to Christ our Lord.
            Amen.

Three Activities for Responding
by Brad Berglund

1. Approach the cross.

Walking up to a large wooden cross set dramatically in the sanctuary is a powerful way for the congregation to remember and connect to the love Jesus showed for each of us as he suffered there. (This cross could be erect or placed on the floor horizontally.) This worshipful act provides a way for us to bring our pain and the pain of the world to Christ in this moment. During a time of response in worship (at least fifteen minutes), invite the congregation to come forward to the cross spontaneously and only as they feel compelled to do so. Have chairs, pillows, prayer benches, kneelers, etc. available for people as they pray. Put index cards and pens around the foot of the cross with nails and hammers in baskets nearby. Give people the opportunity to take a card and write something that needs to be given up to Jesus. Allow them to actually nail that note card to the cross. (This experience may be overwhelming for some. It may be important to have pastors, Stephen's ministers, or others on hand to be of assistance as needed.)

Have Bibles available in case those praying would like to meditate on Scripture. Suggested Scriptures include Psalm 18:2; 23; 51:10; 139:1-6; 139:13-18; Matthew 5:4; 6:24-34; Romans 12:1-2; 2 Corinthians 1:3-7; and 1 Peter 1:3.

2. Create a wailing wall in the sanctuary.

(This act of worship and prayer is especially effective for the entire season of Lent.)

The Western Wall in Jerusalem is an active center of prayer. It is common at the wall to write a prayer, roll it into a small scroll, and place it between massive stones that have been receiving the prayers of God's people since the time of King Solomon. Imagine these stones as the "keepers of memory." What would they reveal about the journey of faithful, praying people through the ages?

Sitting at that wall in Jerusalem, it is easy to see all three aspects of Jesus' Great Commandment—loving God with mind, strength, and heart—being put to use. The mind or thinking center is active in writing and reading prayers, the strength or doing center is active as pray-ers sway and bend low, and the heart or feeling center is present through tears of deep release and lament.

Give your congregation the opportunity to visit the Western Wall by creating one in your sanctuary. This can be as simple as a large piece of cloth draped along the wall with pins provided to attach the prayers or as sophisticated as a plaster wall re-creation of large stones, made to look like the wailing wall itself. Following a short meditation, give people time to write a prayer and invite them to come to the wall. Give them the freedom to kneel, rock, sway, sing, or lament as they place their prayer between the stones.

3. Provide a variety of multisensory ways for people to respond.

On tables or "stations" around the sanctuary, provide the following options for the congregation to respond to the movement of God in their lives and in the life of the congregation. Give worshipers time to move around the room. For those who do not want to move or who cannot move, provide in the bulletin or on the screen something that could include them if they choose.

Station #1: Paper, pencils, and envelopes. We have come to worship to connect deeply with God and with others. Many people have their highest and best thoughts in the context of worship. Give them time to write a letter to someone who needs to hear from them or to pen a letter of thanks, lament, prayer, or friendship to God.

Station #2: Construction paper, colored pens, and colored markers. Many people need to respond to God without the use of words. James Earl Massey tells us, "The heart knows things the mind may never understand." Give people time to express their inner world of symbol, image, color, and shape and to offer that to God.

Station #3: Paper and pens. Journaling is one of the ways the congregation can express their loving response to God. Some people will need to enhance the printed word with colorful or symbolic "extras." Provide stickers, cut-up magazines, other collage materials, glue sticks, and ink-blot stamps.

Station #4: Index cards, pencils, baskets, unlit candles with matches or lighters, and incense with bowls of sand. A prayer table provides a creative way to involve the congregation in the practice of prayer. Invite participants to write a prayer, drop it in the basket, and light a candle or stick of incense as a way of visualizing that prayer "going up to God."

Station #5: Verses of Scripture, pillows, prayer benches, a focal point for prayer, candles, and ancient icons or pictures of the natural world. Give people time to simply sit and meditate on Scripture or quotations from spiritual writers.

Sending

God demands nothing less than complete self-surrender as the price of the only real freedom worth having. And, when we lose ourselves, we immediately find ourselves in the service of all that lives. It becomes our joy and re-creation. We are a new person, never weary of spending ourselves in the service of God's creation.

—Mahatma Gandhi

The word "benediction" means "good speech" or "good word." A benediction sends the congregation into the world to love and serve the least, to encourage and inspire the lonely, to awaken those who are spiritually asleep, and to transform oppressive social structures. The benediction motivates and celebrates. It creates energy and promotes courage. When you offer a benediction, look people in the eye, raise your hands in a sign of blessing, and speak with strength and compassion.

Benediction Offered to One Another

by Brad Berglund

Based on Matthew 5:14, 16

(Tell the congregation they are going to offer the benediction to one another today. Ask them to gather in groups of three or four people. Tell them to take hands, look each other in the eye, and offer this benediction.)

Leader: You are the light of the world.
(Congregation repeats to each other)

Leader: Let your light shine
(Congregation repeats to each other)

Leader: so that others may see your good works
(Congregation repeats to each other)

Leader: and glorify God in heaven.
(Congregation repeats to each other)

Leader: Go in peace!
(Congregation repeats to each other)

Leader: Amen!

Go with Us

by Terry Falla

Lord, as we part and go our different ways,
it is our prayer that you will give us,
each in our own way,
the passion for living and loving,
the courage for daring and hoping,
the freedom for growing and changing,
the capacity for giving and receiving,
the humility for learning,

the tenderness for understanding,
the strength for enduring,
and the trust for believing,
and may your grace and your peace—
which is not the absence of conflict,
but the presence of all that makes life whole—
be with us and go with us. Amen.

The Blessing
by Lois Wilson

The blessing of the God of Sarah, of Hagar, and of Abraham,
the blessing of the Son born of the woman Mary,
the blessing of the Holy Spirit, who broods over us
as a mother over her children,
be with you now and forever.
Amen.

Truth, Hope, Freedom, and Joy
by Terry Falla

May God your Creator, your Redeemer and Sustainer,
be the truth on which your life and death are built,
your hope that cannot be destroyed,
your freedom from which love and justice flow,
and the joy that has eternity within it. Amen.

A Gaelic Blessing

Deep peace of the running wave to you,
deep peace of the flowing air to you,
deep peace of the quiet earth to you,
deep peace of the shining stars to you,
deep peace of the gentle night to you,
moon and stars pour their healing light on you,
deep peace of Christ the light of the world to you.
The deep peace of Christ to you. Amen.

Benediction
by Anne D. Kear

Like a rock, God is under our feet.
Like a roof, God is over our heads.
Like the horizon, God is beyond us.
Like water in a pitcher, God is within us and
    in the pouring out of us.
Like a pebble in the sea, we are in God.
Let us go out and change our world as
    God has changed our lives. Amen.

A Multivoiced Prayer and Lesson of Commitment/Sending Out
by Mona Bagasao

(This prayer is especially appropriate for a service by the water or for baptism.)

(To prepare for this prayer, have water—ice, glasses, and pitchers or bowls filled with water—for the people to share. Have the people sing two or three verses of "Study War No More" ["Down by the Riverside"].)

One Voice:
"Water, water everywhere, but not a drop to drink." Today, Holy God, we are saying, "God's love, God's Word, God's water everywhere," but for some not a drop to drink. How can they hear without someone to spread the Good News? How can they drink without someone to offer them water?

One Voice:
Jesus said, "Everyone who drinks from this water will be thirsty again, but whoever drinks from the water that I shall give will never suffer thirst again. The water that I shall give will be an inner spring, always welling up for eternal life."
    "Sir," the woman said, "give me some of *that* water."

All Singing:
I've got peace like a river, I've got peace like a river,
I've got peace like a river in my soul.
I've got peace like a river, etc.

I've got love like an ocean, etc.

I've got joy like a fountain, etc.

And it's all because of Jesus, etc.

One Voice:
"When I was hungry, you gave me food; when I was thirsty, you gave me a drink of water; when I was a stranger, you took me into your home; when naked, you clothed me." When did we do those things for you, Lord? "I tell you this, anything you did for one of my children here, however humble, you did for me."

All Singing:
Deep and wide, deep and wide,
*   there's a fountain flowing deep and wide. (repeat)*
So high I can't get over it. So low I can't get under it.
*   So wide I can't get around it—can't get away from God's love.*
Deep and wide, etc.

One Voice: Lord, we stand at the edge of your great ocean,
    hiding the lowest, deepest trenches and the highest mountains.
All: Your love is so high we cannot get over it, so low we cannot
*   get under it.*

One Voice: Lord, we look at the sky—as wide as the east is from
    the west.
All: Your love is so wide we cannot get around it.

One Voice: Sometimes my life churns like your ocean in a storm.
All: You lead us beside the still waters.

One Voice: Sometimes my life is like the doldrums. I can't see anything, not even you.

All: Your Spirit comes to stir the water, and I am revived.

One Voice: Sometimes, like Alice in Wonderland, I feel so small that I could drown in a pool of my own tears.

All: Your love shall wipe away all tears.

One Voice: Sometimes I am tasteless, good for nothing.

All: Your Word is all I need to become sweet wine.

One Voice: Do this in remembrance of me.

All: Though we may see your face reflected on your mighty ocean or in a single drop of water, for many your image is reflected only by us, who call ourselves by your name, who were created in your image.

One Voice: Let there be light. Let a vault separate the water from the water. Let the waters be gathered together. Let the waters bring forth living creatures.

One Voice: Let us make a human in our own image.

One Voice: So God created the human in God's image; in the image of God they were created; male and female were created.

All: How can they hear without someone to spread the Good News? How can they drink without someone to offer them water?

(One Voice invites the people to share water with one another, symbolizing their willingness to share the Water of Life in old ways, in new ways, in any way the Spirit leads. People offer glasses of water, touch someone's forehead with water from a bowl, give someone a water bottle, etc. [Suggestion: While sharing is taking place, sing Graham Kendrick's song "Is Anyone Thirsty?"])

(When the sharing time has ended, conclude.)

One Voice: Whoever drinks of the water that I shall give
    will never thirst again.
All: Amen.

Benediction Litany
by Julie Hodge Milcoff

Leader: May the spirit of the Lord be present among you
    as you leave this place.

People: Lord, help us remember what you have done for us.

Leader: May you be a light in this world.

People: Lord, help us bring smiles to people's faces.

Leader: May you have humble hearts and open minds.

People: Lord, help us to share your love for us with others.

Leader: May you be slow to anger and judgment.

People: Lord, help us to follow your example.

*All: May we work together as a community of faith to
    spread God's love to others. We go with joy! Amen.*

Benediction

by Latu Tangulu

I have set before you the Word of Life;

Choose it and we will live.

I have set before you the Word of Truth;

Walk in it and we will not be lost.

May the assurance of God's Word guard your hearts,
minds, and souls as you go out to witness for God's love.

May We Bring God

by Nancy B. Smith

To a world filled with lies,
May we bring the truth of God.

To a world filled with ignorance,
May we bring the wisdom of God.

To a world filled with darkness,
May we bring the light of God.

To a world filled with tragedy,
May we bring the hope of God.

To a world filled with hate,
May we bring the love of God.

To a world filled with the emptiness of self,
May we bring the fullness of God.

As we leave this time of worship,
Let us bring God to every place we go.
Amen.

Benediction

by John Romine

May God's forgiveness help you forgive others.
May's God's mercy inspire you to be merciful to others.
May the peace of God found in Christ Jesus
guide you to bring peace in a sin-torn world.
Empowered by God's Spirit, be Christ's light in a darkened world.
Amen.

seasonal Resources

A Prayer for the New Year

by Cindy Bates

Gracious God, there is so much in life that is good, that is wonderful and true. And with that we also know there is much in life that is difficult and very painful and so hard to understand.

O God, give us your grace that we might appreciate and grasp the wonder of life, the gift of life that we have been given to share here together. And give us grace that we might know that even in times of pain and darkness, your love and care for us promise hope and strength to make it through even our darkest valleys. May we all experience your presence in our lives.

As this new season unfolds its days, and all the possibilities and opportunities of new life are present, help us make good choices— wise decisions—for ourselves and those around us. May we remember lessons that past mistakes have taught us, and may we be as gracious and loving about our own failures as Jesus taught us we should be with others. May we go into the future knowing the blessing of being able to forgive ourselves and others. May we judge all persons with our hearts as well as with our minds.

O God, help us to know peace: peace in the world, so that war
will not be a reality; peace in our homes, so we might live together
in love as we grow and learn together; and peace within our
hearts, knowing that we are becoming the persons you would like
us to be. All this we ask in the name of the Prince of Peace, who
taught us to pray together. Amen.

An Invocation for the Beginning of Holy Week
by Mark Theodoropoulos
(For one voice or responsively)

Creator and Sustainer of all:
you see us at our best and rejoice with us,
and call us to share our best with others;

you see us at our worst and grieve for our falling short,
and offer us your love and the gift of a new day.

You are with us in the vast world around us,
and in the eyes of everyone we meet.

You are with us throughout the week
and throughout the year.

Out of our week, we have set aside this hour
to cherish and celebrate your presence.

Out of our year, we have set aside this week
to remember that most turbulent week:
in the time when you walked among us in Jerusalem,
when you called for the best in us, and suffered the worst from us.

Be with us now in this hour, as in word and song
we celebrate the triumph and mourn the desolation of that week.
We ask this in the name of the one who walked with us then
and walks with us still. Amen.

Palm Sunday Prayer of Dedication
by Nancy E. Hall

God of history—we thank you for sending your Son, Jesus Christ, to dwell among us, living and dying to show us your great love for all humanity.

God of this very day—we thank you for all that we have and all that we are. Please accept the gifts we freely offer in praise of you.

God of the days to come—walk with us in our journey, keep us focused upon the cross, and help us to speak words of love, comfort, and welcome in the name of Jesus.

We offer this prayer in that great name, crying "Hosanna!" Blessed is the one who came among us and lives with us still. Amen.

A Prayer for Maundy Thursday
by Cindy Bates

Gracious God, in the quiet of these moments, in the peacefulness of this sanctuary, please speak to us. We pray we may feel your presence and know that you are near, O God.

This is a night to remember, and in the remembering we pray that we may know the full meaning of these holy symbols that we will share. They represent so much love and forgiveness, so much pain and healing, so much of what is really important in our lives.

May these moments that we share together tonight prepare us for understanding with even more clarity the sacrifice and gift of a Good Friday and the incredible hope of an Easter Sunday.

We come to your table because, like the disciples of old, we need forgiveness, we need words of assurance to bring a sense of clarity and meaning to lives that are often confused and feeling empty.

O God, as we eat the bread and drink from the cup, may there be a personal, meaningful moving of our spirit toward yours. Move us to love more. Move us to sin less. Move us to always believe in the name of the one who first told us about the meaning of the bread and wine.

Easter Sunday Prayer of Invocation
by Nancy E. Hall

Eternal God, may we hear with new ears this morning:
"Behold, I tell you a mystery! We shall not all die, but we shall all be changed, for the trumpet shall sound and the dead shall be raised. For, like Christ, our earthly bodies shall put on immortality and the saying shall be fulfilled:
'Where, O death, is your victory?
Where, O grave, is your sting?'"

Thanks be to you, O God, who dwells with us here this morning, who gives us the victory through Jesus Christ. And as we say "Amen," Lord, we proclaim for all time:
"I know that my redeemer lives!"
Christ is risen!

People: *Christ is risen, indeed!*

Pentecost Prayer of Dedication
by Nancy E. Hall

Lord God, we make these offerings as a pledge of our love and loyalty: to you, and to each other, and to all our sisters and brothers in humanity. We commit ourselves to live in love for all, using our heart, soul, mind, and strength, in the name of Christ our Lord. Grant that your spirit of grace and generosity will move in each of our hearts and catch fire throughout our community. In Jesus' name we pray. Amen.

Ritual for Thanksgiving Worship

by Linda Fischer

(The following is based on a phrase from Rev. John Claypool, the contributor's friend, fellow traveler, and mentor. The phrase is one that Rev. Claypool shared often to express what his trust in God through the challenges of his journey taught him: "Life is gift; despair is presumptuous.")

"Life is gift; despair is presumptuous."
(This phrase may be proclaimed or displayed.)

Please turn to a person or two near you and share:
My tendency to despair happens when _____.
How God helps me remember "Life is gift" is _____.

OR

Using the art materials available, draw or sculpt your remembrance of a despairing time and the way that God restored you, helping you remember that "life is gift."

Unison:
Creator God, we thank you.
We believe your grace is great.
That we *are* who we are,
That we *have* what we have,
are your gifts to us.
For "Life is gift" we give thanks.
May this truth be enough.
Amen.

A Traditional Advent Candle Liturgy

by Heather A. Hood

First Sunday of Advent:

Leader: Jesus said, "I am the Light of the world . . .
People: . . . *whoever follows me will have the light of life and will never walk in darkness."*

Leader: Today we light the candle of hope as we anticipate the coming of Jesus, who is our hope now and forever.
People: "Praise to the God and Father of our Lord Jesus Christ! In his mercy he has given us new birth into a living hope."

Leader: Please pray with me. O God, as we begin this new Advent season, shine the light of your hope into our hearts, that we may bring hope to a world in need of you. We pray in the name of your Son, Jesus, the hope of the world. Amen.

Second Sunday of Advent:

Leader: Jesus said, "I am the Light of the world . . .
People: . . . *whoever follows me will have the light of life and will never walk in darkness."*

Leader: Today we light the candle of peace, knowing that only Jesus can bring true peace to our lives.
People: "Now may the Lord of peace himself give you peace at all times and in every way."

Leader: Please pray with me. O God, as we worship together, plant your Spirit in our hearts so that we may be at peace and share your peace with the world. We pray in the name of your Son, Jesus, the Prince of Peace. Amen.

Third Sunday of Advent:

Leader: Jesus said, "I am the Light of the world . . .
People: . . . *whoever follows me will have the light of life and will never walk in darkness."*

A

Leader: Today we light the candle of joy because the good news of Jesus' birth brings great joy to all people.

People: *"Do not be afraid. I bring you good news of great joy that will be for all the people. Today in the town of David a Savior has been born to you; he is Christ, the Lord."*

Leader: Please pray with me. O God, we know that your coming brings joy that rests deep in our hearts. Let that joy overflow into our world as we live each day for you. We pray in the name of your Son, Jesus, the joy of our desire. Amen.

Fourth Sunday of Advent:

Leader: Jesus said, "I am the Light of the world . . .

People: *. . . whoever follows me will have the light of life and will never walk in darkness."*

D

Leader: Today we light the candle of love because we know that God is love, and he teaches us how to love each other.

People: *"Dear friends, let us love one another, for love comes from God. Everyone who loves has been born of God and knows God."*

Leader: Please pray with me. O God, we love you because we know that in Jesus, you first loved us. As we worship together, plant in us the desire to love you more and share your love with the world around us. We pray in the name of your Son, Jesus, your gift of love to us. Amen.

Christmas Eve:

Leader: Jesus said, "I am the Light of the world. . .

People: *. . . whoever follows me will have the light of life and will never walk in darkness."*

2

Leader: B Today we light our first ~~second~~ candle to remind us of the hope we find in Christ.

3

People: We light a ~~second~~ third candle to remind us that true peace comes from knowing Jesus.

[handwritten: Tonight, we light again our first candle]

Leader: ~~We light a third candle~~ to remind us that Jesus brings joy
to our world.

People: We light a fourth candle to remind us of God's steadfast
love in ~~his~~ gift of Jesus.

All: On this night of nights, *[handwritten: O God,]* may we prepare our hearts for the
coming of your light.

Benediction for Advent

by Nancy E. Hall

Pastor: Let us receive the light, and we will receive God.
People: Let us receive the light and become followers of Christ.

Pastor: Sing, O Word; reveal the joy to us.
People: We are the people of God's love.

Unison: Let us sing, and never cease, to the God of peace above.
Amen.

Practice Hope (First Sunday of Advent)

by Rita Berglund

[handwritten: (insert B)]

Practice hope!
In the midst of loss, hopelessness, and despair.

Practice hope!
By doing the hard work of healing.

Practice hope!
By forgiving again and again and again.

Practice hope!
By planting seeds and trees and new life.

Practice hope!
By reaching out to others who are suffering.

Practice hope!
By cherishing your own life.

Practice hope!
By living in the perspective of God's eternity.

Practice hope!

Practice Peace (Second Sunday of Advent)
by Rita Berglund

(Insert C)

Practice peace!
In nonviolent speech.

Practice peace!
With acts of reconciliation.

Practice peace!
By calming the mind and body.

Practice peace!
Through inviting stillness and active listening.

Practice peace!
By creating beauty.

Practice peace!
By detaching from fear.

Practice peace!
With an awareness of God's abiding presence.

Practice peace!

Practice Joy (Third Sunday of Advent)

by Rita Berglund

(*Insert A*)

(This may be used in conjunction with a reading of Psalm 100.)

Practice joy! *Leader*
In breathing deeply (breathe deeply). *people*

Practice joy!
By reaching wide to open your heart (reach wide).

Practice joy!
With a stomp affirming the dance of our life stories (stomp).

Practice joy!
In a clap of blessing (clap).

Practice joy!
With an "Alleluia" of thanksgiving ("Alleluia!").

Practice joy!
By touching one another in gratitude for community (touch one another).

Practice joy!
By listening deeply to the aliveness of this now (listen).

Practice joy!

Practice Love (Fourth Sunday of Advent)
by Rita Berglund

Insert D

Practice love!
In thought, action, and emotion.

Practice love!
With disciplines that facilitate transformation.

Practice love!
With behaviors that heal relationships.

Practice love!
With respect for the brokenness of self and others.

Practice love!
By nurturing children and cherishing the elderly.

Practice love!
By living into truthfulness.

Practice love!
By fearlessly being Christ in the world.

Practice love!

Practice Christmas (Christmas Eve or Christmas Day)
by Rita Berglund

Practice Christmas!
By inspiring hope.

Practice Christmas!
By working for peace.

Practice Christmas!
By making sounds of joy.

Practice Christmas!
By reaching out with generous love.

Practice Christmas!
By inviting the transformation of your heart.

Practice Christmas!
By spreading the good news of Christ.

Practice Christmas!
With every aspect of aliveness.

Practice Christmas!

Christmas Call to Worship

by Nancy E. Hall
(Based on Isaiah 40 and 60)

Leader: Prepare for God's arrival! Make the road straight and
smooth, a highway fit for our God.
*People: Fill in the valleys, level off the hills, smooth out the ruts,
clear away the rocks.*

Leader: Then God's brilliance will shine and everyone will see it.
*People: Get out of bed, Jerusalem! Wake up. Raise your face to
the sunlight.*

*All: God's bright glory has arrived for all the earth. O come,
let us adore the Christ child!*

Resources for Weddings and Funerals

Marriage Vows

Exchange of Vows 1

Husband:

_____, I offer this vow and solemn promise, before my family and friends, and in the presence of God's great Spirit.

_____, I ask you to be my helper and friend, my lover and wife. And in return, I vow to love you above all others for as long as my lifeblood flows. And I shall do my best to challenge you that you will fulfill your human potential. I promise to take you down roads less traveled in search of truth, dignity, and social justice. And I shall do my best to communicate with you my thoughts and dreams, my joys and sorrows, so that you will always know where I stand. Above all, I shall do my best to love and honor, to trust and believe in you so that you will never ever doubt this commitment.

Wife:

_____, I offer this vow and solemn promise, before my family and friends, and in the presence of God's great Spirit.

_____, I ask you to be my helper and friend, my lover and

husband. And in return, I vow to love you above all others for as long as my lifeblood flows. And I shall do my best to challenge you that you will fulfill your human potential. I promise to take you down roads less traveled in search of truth, dignity, and social justice. And I shall do my best to communicate with you my thoughts and dreams, my joys and sorrows, so that you will always know where I stand. Above all, I shall do my best to love and honor, to trust and believe in you so that you will never ever doubt this commitment.

Exchange of Vows 2

Husband:
Because I believe God has brought us together, I, _____, take you, _____, to be my beloved wife. To give to you, from this day forward, the gift of my tender love. To stand by your side and sleep in your arms. To bring out the best in you always, and to encourage you to reach your full potential. I promise to love and honor you, to encourage you and grow with you, to laugh with you in the good times, to struggle with you in the bad. I will care for you in sickness and in health. I will be faithful to you. This I promise you until one of us lays the other in the arms of God.

Wife:
Because I believe God has brought us together, I, _____, take you, _____, to be my beloved husband. To give to you, from this day forward, the gift of my tender love. To stand by your side and sleep in your arms. To bring out the best in you always, and to encourage you to reach your full potential. I promise to love and honor you, to encourage you and grow with you, to laugh with you in the good times, to struggle with you in the bad. I will care for you in sickness and in health. I will be faithful to you. This I promise you until one of us lays the other in the arms of God.

Exchange of Vows 3

Husband:
I take you, _____, to be my wife. I promise before God and
these friends to be your loving and faithful husband, to share with
you in plenty and in want, in joy and in sorrow, in sickness and
in health. I promise to be a safe place for you in times of fear, and
to keep love alive by giving myself unselfishly. I commit myself
to speak the truth in love even as I listen to you speak the truth
in love to me. I vow to build a loving home, to dream together,
and to walk through the second half of my life with you, so that
together we may serve God and others, as long as we both shall
live. God be my help.

Wife:
I take you, _____, to be my husband. I promise before God
and these friends to be your loving and faithful wife, to share with
you in plenty and in want, in joy and in sorrow, in sickness and
 in health. I promise to be a safe place for you in times of fear, and
to keep love alive by giving myself unselfishly. I commit myself
to speak the truth in love even as I listen to you speak the truth
in love to me. I vow to build a loving home, to dream together,
and to walk through the second half of my life with you, so that
together we may serve God and others, as long as we both shall
live. God be my help.

Exchange of Vows 4

Husband:

I, _____, ask you, _____, to be my partner, my lover, my friend, and my wife. You are an incredibly beautiful human being, and I announce and declare my promise to give you my deepest friendship and love, not only when moments are high, but also when they are low; not only when it is easy, but also when it is difficult. I will challenge you to remember clearly who you are and encourage you to fulfill the best of your potential. I promise before God and those present that I will always seek to see the light of divinity within you and will seek daily to share the light of divinity within me that together we may grow in deepest love, compassion, and maturity. I promise to be with you forever, to love you above all others in a holy partnership of soul, that we may do together God's work, sharing all that is good within us with all those whose lives we touch.

Wife:

I, _____, ask you, _____, to be my partner, my lover, my friend, and my husband. You are an incredibly beautiful human being, and I announce and declare my promise to give you my deepest friendship and love, not only when moments are high, but also when they are low; not only when it is easy, but also when it is difficult. I will challenge you to remember clearly who you are and encourage you to fulfill the best of your potential. I promise before God and those present that I will always seek to see the light of divinity within you and will seek daily to share the light of divinity within me that together we may grow in deepest love, compassion, and maturity. I promise to be with you forever, to love you above all others in a holy partnership of soul, that we may do together God's work, sharing all that is good within us with all those whose lives we touch.

Promises of Shared Dreams and Commitments (When Children Are Involved)
created by Janet and Jeff Savage

(This is an example of how children can be welcomed into a marriage during a wedding ceremony. Whatever the scenario and combination, the important thing is for children of the new partners to be involved in the ceremony that is the primary public ritual of creating this new family. Get the children involved in the planning of the ceremony. Be creative and sensitive to the symbolism of the physical space—where they stand and how movement and action can reinforce their sense of belonging.)

Wife:
(Children's names), I want to thank you for welcoming me into your life and into your home. Change is not easy, and I thank you for sharing yourself with honesty and grace. I promise to love your father, and I look forward to continuing to build a relationship with you as we grow together as a family. I respect you as an amazing, talented (young woman or young man), and promise to encourage and support you in every way I can. I love you.

Husband:
(Children's names), I am so proud to have you standing with me this day. Thank you for your support and love during the difficult changes we have faced together. Thank you for welcoming (wife's name) and for supporting me as I have struggled to keep my heart open to new possibilities. You are each so special to me, and I, as your father, renew my commitment to love you, support you, and stand by you in all that life may bring.

Call to Worship for a Wedding
by Laura Keller

We come together to celebrate our covenant relationship
with God,

A covenant that is lasting and true, full of justice and mercy.

We also celebrate the covenant of marriage that God created
for humankind,

A covenant that is lasting and true, full of patience and generosity.

As God created a human being out of love and adoration,

May we adore and love God our Creator.

As God created a companion and life partner,

*May we be steadfast in all our relationships and offer friendship
and hope to all of God's creation.*

Thanks be to God for the commitment of love we receive and
return.

*All: May we remain true to God's covenant in heaven and our
own on earth.*

Resources for Funerals

Time of Personal Prayer and Reflection during a Funeral
by Jill Kimberly Hartwell Geoffrion

Sample Introduction:
Questions have the ability to bring what is important into focus. They can point us in the right direction. They can offer unlimited possibilities. As I walked alongside my friend through the varying stages of his illness, there were some questions that his life asked me. I began asking these questions as I sat quietly with God.

I am going to share four of these questions. Once I have spoken one, I will pause for about half a minute. I invite you to enter an attitude of prayer. In God's presence, allow each question to take you where it may.

(Note: The word "cancer" may be replaced by a word that more closely describes the reality of the situation.)

Guided Prayer:
From the *earliest* stages of my friend's journey with cancer came this question. In the silence, prayerfully consider: *What changes do I need to make in my life so that I can live more fully?*

(Wait half a minute.)

From the *first half* of my friend's journey with cancer came this question. In the silence, prayerfully consider: *What can I do to make my community a better place, even if I can't do everything that I want to?*

(Wait half a minute.)

From the *second half* of my friend's journey with cancer came this question. In the silence, prayerfully consider: *What do I believe will happen to me after I die?*

(Wait half a minute.)

From the *end* of my friend's journey with cancer came this question. In the silence, prayerfully consider: *In what ways is it time for me to let go and let God?*

(Wait half a minute.)

May these questions, as well as the many other questions that those who have died asked and lived, inspire and nourish us.

Note: The remaining resources in this section, written by Victor D. Lehman, appear in his book *The Pastor's Guide to Weddings and Funerals* (Judson Press, 2001).

A Funeral Invocation
by Victor D. Lehman

Lord of life, author of hope, victor over death, be present with us in these moments of memorial and grant to us the real experience of your living presence. In your infinite and unconditional love, be pleased to look down on our bereaved souls and enable us to hear your holy Word, that through the patience and comfort of the Scriptures, we may again find hope. Impart to our minds an understanding of life after death, to our hearts an assurance of that which we are invited to possess in Jesus Christ, and to our lives the courage to persevere in faithful living. By the power of Jesus Christ, who himself rose from the grave, comfort us and challenge us with the words of eternal life. Amen.

A Prayer for Comfort
by Victor D. Lehman

God, our Father, we thank you for the gift of life and all that makes life precious and worth living. We thank you for choosing to place us in family units, where ties of blood and cords of love draw us close together, especially now in our time of need. Thank you for father love and mother love, for the love of husband, wife, and children.

We thank you, too, for the great friends who have come to stand beside us to strengthen our spirits and enlarge our vision. Life in this community is precious to us, Lord, and today we are conscious that a loved one is no longer part of our community. _____'s (first name) death has served to remind us of how great a gift life really is.

And so we are thankful, God, even in death. We realize that our bodies were not made to last forever. They grow weary and worn out. Thank you that in your design there is provision that when our work is done on this earth and our day is spent, we can be released from these earthly forms, freed from the limitations and weaknesses of the aged human body. Thank you, Lord, that _____ has experienced this release.

Father God, we pray your blessing upon the family and friends of _____. May each of them be provided with the strength and comfort that is needed to sustain them in this hour of sorrow. May we each look to you in faith and receive your gracious support and direction. Amen.

A Prayer of Thanks

by Victor D. Lehman

Thank you, God, for granting _____ the gift of ___ years of life. Each day is indeed a gift from you, and we praise you for this multitude of gifts you granted her/him.

Thank you too for all the relationships that _____ enjoyed. Many of those special people are gathered here today to say farewell to this one whom they loved. Some knew her/him as the beloved matriarch/patriarch of the family. Others knew her/him as Grandma/Grandpa, Aunt/Uncle, or Mom/Dad. Still others experienced her/him as a coworker, a neighbor, a friend. Thank you, Lord of relationships, for the rich ties that bind us to _____.

Lord, we are grateful for the many years of health and vitality with which you blessed _____. Thank you for the good care she/he received to the very end, when her/his health did begin to fail. Thank you for helping _____ to finish well.

And though we are sad today, O Lord, we are also thankful for the many precious memories with which we are left. These memories will live on, far beyond today, continuing to enrich our lives and the lives with whom we share them. We are indeed richer for having known _____, and for this we give you praise. Amen.

A Prayer for Release from Pain
by Victor D. Lehman

Loving Father, we are touched by the memories of those who have just lost a loved one. Memories are indeed a precious gift. Thank you for the gift of families; thank you for love and friendship. Thank you for the long life and experiences you gave _____ and for how she/he touched our lives, whether as father/mother, husband/wife, brother/sister, grandfather/ grandmother, or friend. Thank you for this opportunity to remember and to share those memories.

But, Lord God, we also are experiencing the pain of death and separation. Though we would not wish her/him back to the painful limitations she/he had prior to leaving us, our pain is now real. We will miss her/him. Thank you for meeting us in our grief. Thank you for releasing _____ from his/her pain. Thank you for the healing you will bring through the grief process, healing that will begin to lessen our pain. Thank you for caring loved ones with whom to share this time of sorrow. Thank you for your comforting presence here that brings us hope in the midst of our pain. In Jesus' name. Amen.

Miscellaneous Resources

Lent 2008?

Lent 2010

Eternal Spirit
by Jim Cotter

Eternal Spirit,
Earth-maker, Pain-bearer, Life-giver,
source of all that is and that shall be,
Father and Mother of us all,
loving God, in whom is heaven:

The hallowing of your name echo through the universe!
The way of your justice be followed
by the peoples of the world!
Your heavenly will be done by all created beings!
Your commonwealth of peace and freedom
sustain our hope and come on earth!

With the bread that we need for today, feed us.
In the hurts we absorb from one another, forgive us. *as we forgive others*
In times of temptation and test, strengthen us.
From trials too great to endure, spare us.
From the grip of all that is evil, free us.

134

For you reign in the glory of the power that is love,
now and forever. Amen.

(Alternatively, the first and third stanzas of this contemporary form of the Lord's Prayer may be said by the women, and the second and fourth stanzas by the men, or vice versa.)

For the Earth
by Rebecca Gale

For our physical world, so altered and moved by human hands, and so in need of extraordinary love and care.

Let those of us who have so much invest in the interest of this planet with sustainable, nurturing practices, purchases, and prayers.

Let us treat her as our cherished home so that she may survive and thrive for our children and for generations beyond.

For This Land
by Bill Wallace

God of all creation,
may our senses be awakened to your presence
in the beauty of this land;
may our imagination be awakened to your suffering
in the cries of this land;
may our hearts be awakened to your compassion
in the peoples of this land;
may our consciences be awakened to your commitment
to the poor of this land;
may our whole being be awakened to your Spirit
enfolding this land.
Amen.

Prayer of Commitment to Those Who Are Lonely

by Mona Bagasao

(Suggestion: Begin by playing the song "Casey's Last Ride" by Kris Kristofferson or a similar song.)

Leader: Then the Lord God said, "It is not good that the human should be alone; I will make a helper as a partner" (Genesis 2:18, paraphrase).

One voice: It is not good to be alone.

All: Loving God, we have been alone. But in our loneliness we have felt your presence. You have called us to be together, to be whole, to be integrated with ourselves, with each other, with your created world, with your children—our sisters and brothers who are in political, social, emotional, and spiritual loneliness. It is not good to be alone. It is our shame that others are alone.

Leader: God said, "It is not good that this human should be alone. I will make a companion, a helper, for this one."

All: We have come from loneliness to be companions, to be together. We commit ourselves to wholeness. We commit ourselves to one another. We commit ourselves to you. Amen.

For Those Who Are Abused
by Brad Berglund

For families who suffer the pain of abuse,
give victims the courage and wisdom
to care for themselves and their children.
Give perpetrators the courage and wisdom
to face the truth of their actions.
May opportunities for healing become apparent
to all family members.

Lord, hear our prayer.

For Those Who Are Displaced
by Brad Berglund

We pray for those caught in the crossfire of world politics.
Give our leaders strength and wisdom
in dealing with refugees and migrant people
and all those displaced by violence and injustice.
May they find safety, shelter, and peace.

Lord, hear our prayer.

For Reconciliation
by Michelle Stewart

Many people are out of touch—
out of touch with others,
out of touch with themselves.

Too busy to remember that others exist,
never loving others,
unable to love themselves,
unable to love those hungry for love,
unable to love those lost and friendless.

People are dying for love.
Without love,
people are unable to live.

Those who don't know love need our love;
they want to be filled with love,
never to hunger again.

Peace Prayer
attributed to Francis of Assisi

Lord, make me an instrument of your peace.
Where there is hatred, let me sow love.
Where there is injury, pardon.
Where there is doubt, faith.
Where there is despair, hope.
Where there is darkness, light.
Where there is sadness, joy.
O divine Master, grant that I might seek not so much to be
consoled as to console; to be understood as to understand; not so
much to be loved as to love another; for it is in giving that we now
receive, it is in pardoning that we are now pardoned, and it is in
dying that we are born into eternal life.

For Peace
from the Salisbury Cathedral

O Lord Jesus, stretch forth your wounded hands in blessing over
your people, to heal and restore, and to draw them to yourself
and to one another in love.

Jesus, Save Us
from A New Zealand Prayer Book

Jesus, you saw the world through the eyes of a child.
Save us from the pride that would refuse your command
to live like you in simplicity and joy.

Gathering Prayer for a Group of Artists
by Sue Ellen Echard

O God, we thank you for creating us, artists, in your image.
We ask for the filling of your Holy Spirit, that through our hands
and eyes and voices we may experience the wonders of your love.
May we proclaim the astounding mystery of creation through the
beauty of art in all its forms, and make you known through the
spirit of our creativity, which begins and ends in you. Amen.

Honoring Our Work
by Susan Gillies

(This litany, along with the prayer, is especially appropriate for Labor Day
weekend. Ask members to wear to worship on that Sunday clothing they wear
to work. A connection between everyday work and worship is made when the
congregation sees the offering being taken by a postal worker, Communion
being offered by a pharmacist, a solo sung by a law enforcement officer, etc.)

Leader: We come from the world of work to this place
of worship.
People: Gracious God, bless us, we pray.

Leader: Thank you for those who carry the light of your love
into their work in healthcare.
People: Gracious God, grant them wisdom.

Leader: Thank you for those who live their faith while working
in commerce and industry.
People: Gracious God, grant them courage.

Leader: Thank you for those who show your grace in
educational settings.
People: Gracious God, teach them patience.

Leader: Be present with those who have not found fulfilling work.
People: Gracious God, may they be assured of your love.

Leader: For all who work at home, serve in churches,
or are retired,
People: *Gracious God, bless them with joy.*

Leader: In our daily lives, whether stress-filled, rewarding,
challenging, or routine, may we find our ministry.
People: *Gracious God, show us your way.*

Prayer:
God of builders, artists, teachers, software designers, and
pediatricians, we bring the concerns of our daily lives to you.
What sounds good on Sunday is often hard to live out on
Monday. Grant us the strength to be witnesses through the quality
of our work, our caring, our values, our ethics. May we address
challenges and conflicts in ways that reflect your love in our lives.
Help us become all you created us to be.

Benediction:
"For I know the plans I have for you," declares the LORD, "plans
to prosper you and not to harm you, plans to give you hope and
a future" (Jeremiah 29:11, NIV).

Ask particular groups of "workers" to stand, and say to
them, "Your work is important to God. Hear these words of
encouragement: To you, computer programmers, God says,
'I have plans for you, plans to prosper you and not to harm
you, plans to give you hope and a future.'"

Groups will inevitably be left out. At the end, ask all those who
remain seated to stand. Say to them, "Whatever your work is,
it is important to God. Hear these words of encouragement:
To you, God says, 'I have plans for you, plans to prosper you and
not to harm you, plans to give you hope and a future.' Amen."

Salt and Light
by Kerry Greenhill
(A choral reading based on Matthew 5:13-16)

All: You are the salt of the earth.

1, 3, 5: *(asking others)* Me? Really?

2, 4, 6: Yes! You are the salt of the earth!

1: Mm, salty.

2: Tasty.

3: *(know-it-all)* . . . and important for preserving food!

4–6: But if salt has lost its taste, how can its saltiness be restored?

(all look at each other, confused)

1: I don't know. Can it?

2, 4: It is no longer good for anything,

3: Ick! *(makes face)*

2, 4: but is thrown out and trampled underfoot.

(all mime tossing salt over shoulder, then shrug)

All: You are the light of the world.

1–3: *(pointing out to congregation)* YOU

4–6: are the LIGHT of the WORLD!

5: *(stage whisper)* All of them?

6: *(stage whisper)* Are you sure?

(4 nods vigorously)

5: A city built on a hill cannot be hid.

6: Well, duh!

4: Yeah, cities tend to stand out anyway.

6: Especially on top of a hill.

1, 5: No one after lighting a lamp puts it under a bushel basket,

3: Silly goose.

1, 5: but on the lampstand,

3, 4: and it gives light to all in the house.

2: In the same way,

1–5: let your light shine before others,

6: *(wasn't paying attention)* What?

2, 3: Let your light shine.

1, 4: Let your light

5: SHINE!

6: Shine?

1–5: LET YOUR LIGHT SHINE!

6: Where?

1–5: *(one after another, overlapping)* Let your light shine before others!

1, 2: Before others.

3, 4: Before others.

6: Oh!

All: *Let your light shine so that others may see your good works and give glory to your Father in heaven.*

1: You are the salt of the earth.

2: *(to 3)* What if salt loses its flavor?

(3 shrugs)

4: You are the light of the world.

5: Don't hide it under a bushel basket.

6: Let your light shine.

3: *(raises hand)* Wait, why was that again?

2: So that others may see your good works

4: and give glory to God.

3: *(nodding)* Oh, right.

1: Be salty!

5: Shine brightly!

4: Do justice!

2: Love mercy!

3, 6: Walk humbly with God!

All: *LET YOUR LIGHT SHINE!*

About the Contributors

Several contributors originally wrote their pieces for a class called Worship in Free Church Traditions taught by Professor Nancy Hall at American Baptist Seminary of the West in Berkeley, California. The following persons had their contributions selected for this resource: Phyllis Butt, Patricia Ciupek-Reed, Antonia L. Jones-Wynn, Laura Keller, Moon Louie, Julie Hodge Milcoff, Elane O'Rourke, Kristen Preston, John Romine, Albirda Rose-Eberhardt, Bran Scott, Nancy B. Smith, Latu Tangulu, and Mark Theodoropoulos.

Contributions (used by permission) from the following persons first appeared in the 1994 book *Be Our Freedom, Lord* (Open Book Publishers, Adelaide, South Australia): Alan Boezak, Jim Cotter, Alan Gaunt, Werner and Lotte Pelz, Michelle Stewart, Bill Wallace, and Lois Wilson.

Mona Bagasao is chaplain/director of Campus Ministries at Eckerd College in St. Petersburg, Florida. She is a church musician and writes the art interpretation for *The Upper Room* magazine. Contact her at bagasaom@eckerd.edu.

Cindy Bates has been a United Methodist pastor for more than twenty years. She is currently serving as the senior associate pastor at St. Andrew U. M. Church in Highlands Ranch, Colorado, where she specializes in adult education and spiritual formation. Contact her at cbates@st-andrew-umc.com.

Rita Berglund, MA, leads retreats and teaches courses in human development and spiritual practice at the Iliff School of Theology in Denver and Naropa University in Boulder, Colorado. She is also a psychotherapist who works with individuals and families in a private practice. Contact her at rita@illuminatedjourneys.com.

Karen Berry, OSF, is a Franciscan sister living in Tucson, Arizona. She is the director of a program of family religious education at St. Frances Cabrini parish and a freelance teacher of adult religious formation programs in the diocese of Tucson.

Sally M. Brower, PhD, is a Lutheran pastor trained as an artist, psychologist, and spiritual director. As a parish pastor, retreat leader, and author, she helps people awaken to the mystery of God, risk holy encounter, and cross the thresholds of their hearts' deep hopes. Contact her at sbrowerphd@aol.com.

Krysia Bereday Burnham is a writer and MDiv student at Andover Newton Theological School in Newton, Massachusetts. Her work has appeared in such publications as the *New York Times Book Review*, *Vogue*, *Town and Country*, and *European Travel and Life*. Contact her at krysiaburnham@rcn.com.

Cynthia Cearley has served as an ordained Presbyterian pastor for twenty-eight years. Currently she serves as a copastor at Denver's Montview Boulevard Presbyterian Church. She shares in worship leadership, pastoral care, and program support with her colleagues. Contact her at cearley@montview.org.

Robert and Susan Davis live with their two teenage sons in Denver, Colorado. **Susan** is a full-time mother, occasional artist and musician, and lifelong learner. **Robert** is an accomplished musician who plays guitar, mandolin, hammered dulcimer, and piano. A professional chef, Robert speaks French and has traveled widely throughout Europe. Contact them at www.voila-chef.com or susan@voila-chef.com.

Theodorre Donson and his spouse, Kathy Hurley, are spiritual teachers and international leaders in developing the Enneagram. Their research into the Desert Elder tradition and their living this spirituality informs all their work, as does their close involvement with their children and grandchildren. Contact them at www.hurleydonson.com.

M. Ingrid Dvirnak is the consulting editor for *Judson Bible Journeys for Adults*, published by Judson Press, and the editor of the regional newsletter of the American Baptist Churches of the Rocky Mountains. Her passion is the ministry of the written word. Contact her at idvirnak@abcrm.org.

Sue Ellen Echard is director of music and arts at the Church of the Holy Spirit in Harleysville, Pennsylvania. She earned bachelor of music and bachelor of science degrees at Philadelphia College of Bible and a master of sacred music degree at Westminster Choir College. Contact her at sueellenechard@yahoo.com.

Terry Falla is a research scholar and director of the Syriac Language Research Centre at Whitley College, Melbourne. He is a Baptist minister and has been a lecturer in Old Testament studies in Melbourne and Auckland. He is editor of the award-winning book of contemporary prayers *Be Our Freedom, Lord*, from which some selections in this resource are drawn. Terry and his wife, Berris, have four children and eight grandchildren. Contact him at tfalla@whitley.unimel .edu.au.

Linda Fischer, PhD, is in private practice as a marriage and family therapist in Centennial, Colorado, after practicing in pastoral counseling settings in Texas and Colorado. In her work she helps persons move toward transformation in mind, body, and spirit as well as in relationship. Contact her at lindafischer@mindspring.com.

Rebecca Gale is a singer/songwriter who has cultivated and shared her love of music through choral and solo performance, her leadership of Taizé-style contemplative prayer services, and her hospice music therapy. Contact her at www.RebeccaGale.com.

Jill Kimberly Hartwell Geoffrion, PhD, is the author of seven books on the labyrinth. As artist-in-residence at DeepHaven Labyrinths and Retreats, she encourages others through retreats and consultations to combine contemplative spirituality with creative expression. Contact her at www.jillkhg.com.

Susan Gillies, MA, is executive minister of the American Baptist Churches of Nebraska. Contact her at sgillies@abcnebraska.com.

Kerry Greenhill is pursuing ordination as a deacon in the United Methodist Church, focusing on young adult ministry, justice and peace issues, and worship leadership through liturgical art. Contact him at kerrygreenhill@hotmail.com.

Nancy E. Hall, DMin, is associate professor of ministry at American Baptist Seminary of the West, Berkeley, California. A church musician for most of her life, Nancy has served as an instructor of worship and as director of contextual education at ABSW. She co-authored, with the late John E. Skoglund, *A Manual of Worship* (Judson Press, 1993).

Desmond Hoffmeister is transitional executive minister of the American Baptist Churches of the Rocky Mountains. Contact him at dhoffmeister@ abcrm.org.

Heather A. Hood serves as the minister of Worship and Music at Christ Presbyterian Church in Edina, Minnesota, where she has been on the staff since 1985. She is a 2003 graduate of the Institute for Worship Studies, receiving a doctor of worship studies degree. Contact her at heather@cpconline.org.

Patricia L. Hunter, DMin, is a regional member service representative with the American Baptist Churches' Ministers and Missionaries Benefit Board. She also serves as an associate minister at the Mount Zion Baptist Church in Seattle, Washington. Contact her at plhunter@msn.com.

Anne D. Kear serves as senior minister of First Congregational United Church of Christ in Longmont, Colorado. Worship that is inclusive of all and that welcomes diversity is important to her ministry, which reflects her commitment to justice, peace, and the whole earth. Contact her at revannek@ecentral.com.

Victor D. Lehman is lead pastor at First Baptist Church in Fargo, North Dakota, and the author of the Judson Press books *The Pastor's Guide to Weddings and Funerals* and *The Work of the Pastor.*

Michael-Ray Mathews, MDiv, serves the congregational community at Grace Baptist Church in San José, California. He is committed to creative and inspired multicultural, intergenerational, justice-seeking ministries. Contact him at pastor@gracechurchsj.org.

Charlotte Million has enjoyed a thirty-year career in marketing communications, primarily in higher education. She provides consulting and writing through her company, Million Creative, and serves as director of marketing communications for the University of Colorado at Denver and Health Sciences Center.

John Pipe, MDiv, is a retired American Baptist pastor who has served as an interim pastor in the Denver area. He worships a God of surprises and is open to being surprised in the worship of God! Contact him at johnpipe610@msn.com.

Russell Rathbun is the author of *Post-Rapture Radio: Lost Writings from a Failed Revolution at the End of the Last Century* (Jossey-Bass, 2005). One of the preachers at House of Mercy Church, he lives in St. Paul, Minnesota, with his wife and two children. Contact him at russell@houseofmercy.org.

Brother Roger of Taizé (Brother Roger Schutz) was the leader of the Taizé Community in France for more than forty years. Each midday, at the end of the silence that followed the Bible reading, Brother Roger said a prayer that he'd written for that day. Roger died in August of 2005.

Deana Schneider coordinates a monthly service in the style of the Taizé Community at Calvary Baptist Church of Denver. She also has led mandala workshops and retreats throughout the Front Range area of Colorado. Contact her at deana_schneider@msn.com.

Joni Seivert directs Connections Unlimited LLC, a network of providers of in-home services and products (www .jonisconnections .com). He is also cofounder of the *Alliance for Holistic Aging*, a national membership nonprofit focusing on incubating new ways of aging successfully for the boomer generation and their families. Contact him at www.holisticaging.org.